My Early Life in the Lost River Valley

by

Roland C. Lindburg

Compiled by
Karen Lindburg Gustafson

Lucky Boy Press

My Early Life in the Lost River Valley
Second Edition, 2015

Lucky Boy Press, Boise, Idaho

Copyright © 2005, 2015 Karen Lindburg Gustafson

First Edition, 2005; Karen Lindburg Gustafson, Wayne Gustafson, Mac Tschanz, editors
Second Edition, 2015; Paula Green Gustafson, editor

Quantity discounts are available to organizations dedicated to preserving Idaho history. Contact info@luckyboypress.com for information.

Cover photo: © Leland Howard,
www.finestnaturephotography.com

Map courtesy of Jonathan Norred

ISBN: 978-0-692-38112-0

Introduction

This collection of stories is about a boy growing up in Idaho's Lost River Valley in the early 1900s. Roland Lindburg writes of his birth, his childhood years, and of working as a young man during the Great Depression. He tells a colorful story of family life of that era, his school and athletic endeavors, and of his family's evolution from farming to trucking. Their trucking business, the Lindburg Truck Line, delivered them into places and situations that are interesting from both historical and human perspectives.

Later in life, when he couldn't physically continue some of his favorite activities, Roland began writing. Without research and strictly from memory, he pecked away on a word processor and later on a computer. He died in 2000 at the age of 86. Because of his death, these memories end with the big haul of a dredge into Yankee Fork; but it was shortly after this event that he married and left the Lost River Valley. His children and grandchildren collaborated to transfer his writings into book form.

Thanks for the memories, Dad.

—Karen Lindburg Gustafson

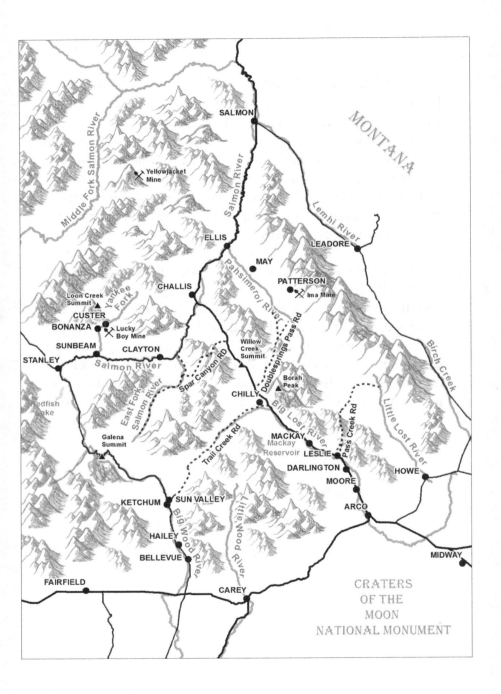

My Earliest Years

I was born February 4, 1914 to Cecil B. Lindburg and Marie Nelson Lindburg. I don't remember the first two years of my life, but on February 2, 1916 my brother, Geryl, was born. Six months later my mother passed away, so I don't have any memory of her at all.

Some might wonder how I happened to be born in Idaho, when all the rest of the Lindburgs lived in Nebraska. It seems as though a real estate broker in Nebraska had a listing on quite a large tract of land in the Lost River Valley of Idaho, at a place called Darlington[1]. And, he was trying to interest my Grand-dad, William Lindburg, his brother-in-law Frigit Carlson, and a friend, Charley Olson, into going out and looking it over to see if they would be interested in buying some of it. So, they came to Idaho and looked the situation over. It must have impressed my Granddad, and it must have been a good farming year in Nebraska, because they ended up buying 280 acres of ground two miles west of Darlington. Frigit Carlson bought 80 acres of land right at Darlington. Charley Olson bought the old Darlington place that was well developed with a lot of buildings on it, and also the 80 acres between my Granddad's place and Frigit Carlson's place.

My Granddad was going to move to Idaho and take Grandma and their youngest son, Maurice (I knew him as Morris) with him, but when he got back to Nebraska, Grandma refused to go. Dad was their oldest son and newly married, so

---

[1] Cecil was married in 1911, so this would have been sometime during 1911 or 1912. The real estate broker was, in fact, Cecil's uncle.

Granddad persuaded him to go. Dad was pleased because he wanted to get out of Nebraska.

Now, I remember the family telling about how my Granddad stood up on a butte that was on the farm that he bought, and he looked over the land and said, "This is a Garden of Eden." But, it didn't turn out that way.

Mother passed away in April 1916 (she died in Pocatello, Idaho, in the hospital; I don't know what her ailment was, as I was never told), and she was taken back to Nebraska for burial. My grandmother, Josephine Lindburg, came to Idaho and took Geryl and me home to Nebraska and we lived with her for about three years.

Life with My Grandparents in Polk

In my grandparents' family were Grandmother, Granddad, and their daughters, Josephine and Evelyn. I don't remember much about their son Maurice being around there, but I guess he was. Or, maybe he was married. I don't remember. Granddad was very fond of children and he would take Geryl and me and our cousins, William and Margaret (children of Dad's brother, Eleanor), to town almost every afternoon. We would always get treats, candy, etc. By the time we would get home, our appetites were spoiled and we had a hard time eating supper. Grandma would reprimand Granddad every day about that. Of course, we liked the treats.

I can remember that it got cold in Nebraska in the wintertime when the automobiles would not run and everyone would move around with buggies. Granddad had a real fancy buggy, a real fancy team, and big, heavy horsehide robes. We would all bundle up and drive to church in Polk on Sunday morning. This buggy was a two-seater so I felt very honored to get to ride in the front seat with Granddad. Granddad lived about a mile north of Polk, so the ride wasn't too long, but it seemed quite a distance in the cold. If it got too cold, we would be clear under the covers.

My first clear recollection was when Armistice Day was celebrated in Polk—and it was a real celebration. Everyone went to town and set off fireworks. I remember that very plainly. The next event I can remember well was the marriage of my Aunt Jo (Josephine) to a fellow named Herb Wurst. She was married at Grandpa's house and Geryl was a ring bearer. There was a crowd and it was quite a show. I can remember Dad and his brothers, Willard and Maurice, teasing Herb about being mixed up with the Lindburgs. It didn't bother Herb. The Lindburgs were all Swedes, and Herb was a German who lived south of Polk in the German community. But, he was accepted into the family and it turned out that he was a swell guy.

My next memory was of Uncle Eleanor being sick and that he passed away of TB (tuberculosis). I thought it was TB, but afterwards I found out that he had another infection that caused his death. He died in Colorado, at a place that had good therapy for TB. My grandmother stayed there with him.

Dad Takes a Wife

Then my dad married again, in about 1919, to a woman named Mabel Viktoria Hult. I think I was about five years old. Then we moved to Harvard, Nebraska, where I started school in a little old country schoolhouse when I was six.

We moved again and I went to school south from Harvard toward Clay Center. The school was farther from home than before. Dad had an old gray horse and said I could ride him to school. He looked like a horse that you see in cartoons—his backbone was like a two by four with the ribs sticking out of the bottom of it. On the way, there was a row of trees and, no matter how hard I pulled on the reins, he would get over into those trees and brush me off. Then he would go home and I would walk on to school—then walk home. It was about two miles to school from home. I also remember that I was in a Christmas program and I sang a song, something about "apples for a penny." I suppose I looked like Alfalfa in the Our Gang comedy.

Later in the year, a family that lived closer to the school had a daughter and she walked to school all the time. They asked if she could ride horseback with me. That was fine because I thought that maybe she could keep him out of the trees. She couldn't. The horse still got into the trees and raked us both off.

I remember the time that Mom was doing some canning and sent Geryl and me down to Aunt Ruth Aker to get some vinegar. Back then, syrup came in pails with bails on them with a press-on lid. She had a half-gallon syrup pail. She put a rope

though the bail and the rope went around Geryl's neck. I rode the horse and Geryl was on behind, hanging onto me with the pail hanging down the side. We arrived at Akers with no problem and got the vinegar. We started home and along the way saw my uncle, Parks Aker, plowing a field with a big oil-pulled tractor. We thought it would be nice just to wait there until he came to the end and

Geryl and Roland

turned around. When he got close to us the tractor scared the horse, we fell off, and the horse stepped on the vinegar pail. Only our feelings were hurt, I guess. Both of us got up and Uncle Parks came over and stopped the tractor to see if we were okay. Then we returned to our aunt's house, and she took us home along with a glass jar of vinegar, and everything was fine.

Life in Danbury

The next move my folks made was to Danbury, Nebraska. That was the most desolate place we lived and I just hated it. We were there for two or three years, until 1924 or 1925, and I went to school in town. A school bus picked us up when the weather was good but it couldn't run when the weather was bad, so we had to find another way to school. That school was a rough and tough place, but I survived. The high school kids played basketball, and the basketball court was outdoors. The floor was smoothly leveled bare ground, and on Friday afternoons, school would let out early and we would all go around to watch the basketball games. I don't think there was a football team. But we had fun playing jacks and marbles. Marbles were a big thing in those days and I was not very good at it, so I stayed out of games that were played for keeps. Times were tough and I didn't have money to buy many marbles. I really valued those that I had and kept them. To this day, I'm no gambler.

While at Danbury, we had a dry-land farm and didn't have good crops. They would start out good, but hail storms or some other pestilence would come. Dad had a good field of grain that was nearly ripe when locusts came through and destroyed it. A pitchfork was left out and was pitted where the locusts chewed it. I left a jacket out and all that was left of it was the buttons. When they came through, that was the end of the crops.

We grew corn and, once in a while, we had a good crop. But, when the crop was good, the price was down. Because there was no wood near Danbury, which was on a prairie, we burned coal. Corn was cheaper than coal one year, so we burned it. It made a hot fire and beat coal when it came to fuel. Otherwise, when corn was priced high enough, it would be shelled and we would burn the cobs. One of my jobs was to keep the cob box full and that was hard because the cobs didn't last long once they got into the stove.

Dad bought a threshing machine and an Avery tractor—a brand new outfit. I think he bought it back in Polk from the Ricestroms. I believe my Granddad had some interest in the Ricestrom Implement Company because they sold Averys and every one of the Lindburgs had Avery tractors. So, Dad did a lot of threshing around Danbury. A lot of it was in bundles and some of them were harvested with a header.

I can remember when they threshed at our place; Mom had to feed the threshing crew. That required a lot of help from Geryl and me. When Mom needed butter, we churned our own. The churn was a barrel on an axle with a paddle that was hand turned, and the cream would drop from one end to the other. Well, on that day I churned and churned. I looked through the little glass peek-hole in the lid; the glass was still white. When the butter was churned, the buttermilk would wash the glass off and then you could see into the churn. When the glass was clear, then you knew it was butter. Because I was sure that it had to be butter, I undid the bail and looked inside. It was still cream so I put the lid back on but didn't get the bail on right. I turned the churn back over, the lid fell off, and the cream spilled on the floor. Getting a meal ready for a threshing crew and having cream all over the floor didn't set well with Mom, so I guess I suffered the consequences.

When I was about eight years old Dad taught me to drive because Mom didn't drive and he needed someone to run the errands. He didn't teach me too much. My main job was to bring afternoon refreshments out to the harvest crew. Mom would fix them and we would all get into the car and take off for the threshing outfit. The refreshments consisted of lemonade, cookies, and things like that. The weather got hot in Nebraska in the summertime.

I was a good driver, I thought. One room of the house extended further than the rest and we kept the 1924 Model T car sheltered there. We also had a 1914 Ford that had a crank instead of a starter and I learned to drive on it. The transmission was in the back, so by jacking up the hind wheels it was easier to crank. Geryl and I would jack up the back wheels and I would turn the crank while he was back there pulling on the wheel. One afternoon Mom wanted to go down to the church in Danbury, which was about two-and-a-half miles from where we lived. I backed out of the parking place, started forward, lost control of the car, and hit a telephone pole that was in front of the house. Mom was thrown into the windshield and banged her forehead. The old car wasn't hurt, but my feelings were. I wasn't punished, but I felt bad about it.

We had a wooden washing machine that had to be pulled by hand. The stick on it moved back and forth. Dad put the washer in a little shack next to the house, and it was my job to pull the handle on the washer when Mom was washing. Well, there was a pulley on it that you could run to a belt. Dad had a Fairbanks engine, so I decided to hook it up to the washing machine. He said it was up to me to keep the engine running because he was out with the threshing crew quite a lot and wasn't home. And, that I would have to keep it running or else pull the stick. I became a pretty good mechanic with that old Fairbanks engine. Anything was better than pulling that stick. I'd rather crank the engine half a day than pull on the stick for an hour. That was my first experience at keeping a machine going. I've been at it ever since.

The house didn't have a bathroom (very few places did in those days), but every Saturday we took a bath whether we needed one or not. That was done with a washtub on the floor in front of the stove, with no change of water. The youngest child started and the oldest was the last, so I don't know how clean I got by the time everybody else finished with their baths. After Dad married Mabel, I had two more brothers, Hilmer and Duane. Dad felt he couldn't stay in Nebraska much longer.

The Move Back to Idaho

Dad went to the Lost River Valley in Idaho one summer[2] and left us in Nebraska. He drove in the Model T Ford that he bought in 1924. I think that car cost him $300 and some. He drove out and came back on the train. He then loaded everything on a boxcar and Mom and us kids went back to Polk to stay until he got to Idaho. After he arrived, he sent a postcard saying that he was ready for us to come. I remember that my cousins, Jim and Junior, were just little fellows so I must have been about 10 years old.

Grandpa took us to Central City, Nebraska, and put us on a train. We were in a sleeper car and arrived in Pocatello the next morning. We had to change trains to go to Blackfoot, which is about 50 miles north of Pocatello and was served by the Yellowstone Railroad. So, I guess we rode the old Yellowstone Special from Pocatello to Blackfoot. Then we got on a

---

[2] The summer of 1924.

branch line that went up into the Lost River Valley, which was about 90 miles away. I think we spent the night in Pocatello with the Selfs. Mrs. Self was Dad's cousin and I think Mr. Self worked for the railroad. Early the next morning they took us back to town and put us on the train. It was quite a ride.

It was all desert until we got to Arco. We then went up through the valley, which had mountains with forests on both sides. It was a dry year and everything, of course, was kind of desert looking. Mom said to the conductor, "I wonder when we will to get to this place they call the Garden of Eden?"—and about five miles later we were in Darlington. Dad met us at the railroad; there was no depot. The train stopped and let people off, and loaded up people who wanted to go on to Mackay. The end of the line was at Mackay, which was about 13 miles up the Valley.

Dad couldn't take possession of the place that Grandpa had bought because there was a renter on it, so we spent the first few months in a vacant log cabin, which was just one room with a loft. It was still standing when Dutch (my brother Duane) and I were there in 1995. We were crowded. We kids, Hilmer, Geryl, and I slept up in the loft. Duane slept down with the folks. There was a well outside, but it had no pump. There was a bucket with a rope, so, when you wanted water, you put the bucket down in the well, got the bucket full, and then hauled it up with the winch. Our refrigeration was a bucket in the corner of the well where we put the butter, cream and other food that we wanted to keep cool.

We milked a few cows and the place had quite a bit of pasture and some alfalfa. So, Dad got an Indian pony that we called Babe, but we couldn't afford a saddle. It was my job to keep the cattle out of the alfalfa. I would be playing in the house and Mom would say, "The cattle are getting in the alfalfa. You had better go get them out." So, I'd get on old Babe and away we would go. The horse knew how to herd and cut cattle, but I didn't. She cut them so sharply that I would fall off. Then she would come back, wait, and want me to get on again. I would find a ditch so I could mount her, and we would try to get the cattle out of the alfalfa again. It got monotonous falling off that horse. I finally learned to hang on. We never did use a bridle, just a rope around her neck. Still, she knew what to do. She was good with kids, and when we were in the corral, she would come to nuzzle us. She felt like she was one of the family, I guess.

There was a nice, new house across the road, which was made of plaster. When the people living there moved out, Dad arranged for us to move into it for the winter. It was a good thing he did because it was a very hard winter. Then in the spring, with the renter gone, we moved to the place where I was born and Dad farmed.

The Lindburgs were all farmers, I guess, but some of them weren't very good farmers and Dad was one of them. He didn't like farming. He liked mechanical work—like building a bridge down at Lost River, or repairing an engine for someone who didn't understand why it wouldn't run—things like that.

The Way We Lived

We had a team of big gray horses. And we had some pretty good crops there, too, but the prices were no good. The sheep we raised helped us more than anything else. We always had 150 to 200 head of sheep and that was our mainstay. I remember one year that Dad had barley that went 90 bushels per acre, but there was no price for it. So, he got some hogs and we fed hogs and sheep. In the spring, he would shear the sheep. The Logan Woolen Mills would take our wool and for half of the wool they would give us back blankets and lots of good warm wool clothing. That was good because we really needed those things in that country. We always had plenty of meat because we raised cattle and hogs. And beans were cheap, so we had plenty of beans. There was an abundance of fish, especially when they drained the water out of the canal. The fish would be trapped in the canals so we'd get pitchforks and catch them. We dried some and smoked some because there were so many. Consequently, fish isn't my favorite food any more. We had potatoes two or three times a day because Dad always planted about half an acre and we had a spud cellar. We always grew a garden so we always had root vegetables like carrots and beets. We put them in the cellar and ate them all year long. About the only food we had to buy were eggs and staples. That is the way we got by when I was a kid.

It was a problem keeping food in those days because we didn't have refrigerators or freezers like we have today. We always did our butchering in the fall and late fall (as we would say) and had to process all of the meat ourselves. Mom made a lot of sausage, which was about half beef and half pork. It was cooked and then kept in a crock of lard through the summer. We also canned a lot of meat. Most winters were cold enough that we hung meat on the north side of the house and it stayed frozen, so we had fresh meat in the winter. But, in the summer we ate mostly canned meat. I don't remember buying any canned goods from the grocery store. We just canned everything out of the garden: peas, beans, and the like.

On a typical day in the summertime we would get up about five o'clock in the morning. Geryl and Dad would milk the cows and I would go out and change the water. Then I would bring in the horses so we could work throughout the day. Horses did everything, as we didn't have a tractor. There were a few tractors around but they were mostly used for threshing— hardly any were used for plowing like we see today. Jobs in the summer were mostly irrigating until haying season—all of the haying was done with horses. I ran the mower from the time we first came to Idaho until we started the truck line. A team of horses was on the mower, which had a six-foot sickle attached. I would mow and Geryl would run the side-delivery rake and rake the hay into windrows. Then we used a dump rake and made the windrows into shocks. Everything was pitched up with pitchforks, whether on the hayrack or else on slips. The slips had slings underneath, so the slips were loaded and we would go alongside the stack. The slings were unloaded there. That's how haystacks were made. It was quite a job. We got one good cutting, and then in the fall we got a second cutting that wasn't quite as heavy as the first. Today farmers want a lot of protein in the hay and cut it before the alfalfa blooms, but in those days we let the hay bloom before we ever cut it. Then we stacked it a little bit on the green side, not so green that it would get hot and burn, but just so it would turn a tobacco color. The cows just went wild over it. Then in the evenings we would come in for supper. After supper the cows were milked and I would go out and set the irrigation water for the night. If we had any extra time then, we could use it for whatever we wanted. We kids usually had games that we played.

The mosquitoes were awfully busy in the summertime. I don't think the Environmental Protection Agency would approve of the way we controlled them in those days. Dad would take a team of horses, some straw and put little piles of straw all the way around the house. Then he would set them on fire. The mosquitoes didn't care much for the smoke, but we lived in the smoke to get away from the mosquitoes. We wore big handkerchiefs underneath our hats, so we could shake our heads to get the mosquitoes off our faces and necks—anything to keep from being bitten. We had nose baskets made of screen on the horses to keep the mosquitoes out of their noses while we were working. I guess the horses kept them off themselves when we weren't working.

Along about the first fifteen days into September we would get a frost. We harvested our grain in September. We grew good grain—some wheat, but mostly barley. We ground it for feed and grinding was my job in the winter. We had an old Model T engine hooked to a Burr grinder and it was set next to the granary. I would feed the grain by bucket into a hopper on the grinder, and then I would put the ground grain into another bin, and we fed the livestock out of that.

In the winter we needed fuel. Because we didn't grow corn and there was no wood in the valley, we always went to the mountains to get wood, using a team of horses and a sleigh. Dad and I generally went four or five miles up to Sheep Creek. We cut pine trees, loaded them onto the sleigh, and hauled them home. Of course, we had no chain saws. All we had was a two-man saw, so we cut the tree down with the two-man saw, then sawed it small enough to get on the sleigh. When we got home, Dad and I would use the saw and cut up chunks small enough to go in the stove. Then Dad split some wood to fit in the kitchen stove. Some of the trees were a couple of feet in diameter, which was a lot of wood, and it was hard work cutting them down. Sometimes it was really cold, so we walked in the mountains to keep warm. I remember coming home in the evenings when the moon would be shining brightly through the dark, and we would be coming out of the mountains with the sleigh, a team of horses and a load of wood. I've seen pictures of the sleighs in the wintertime, and the pictures make it look a lot better than it was.

We also had to feed the cattle and take hay in from the haystack to the yards where we kept the cattle and the sheep. That

13

was an everyday job too, but Dad took care of most of that while we were in school. We would get up early and, of course, do the chores. There was no irrigating then, so I helped milk the cows, which I didn't like, but I didn't have any choice. We milked the cows, fed the calves, had breakfast, got ready, and walked to school.

School in Darlington

The school was more than a mile from where we lived. All of the kids walked or rode horses. There was a barn at the schoolhouse so kids who came quite a distance could put their horses in the barn to keep them out of the weather. The barn was well stocked with hay.

The school consisted of two rooms that were heated with two potbellied stoves—one in each room. The first four grades were in one room and fifth, sixth, seventh, and eighth grades were in the other. A bucket of drinking water, which was kept in the hall, came from a well close to the school. The bucket had a dipper and everybody used it, but nobody seemed to get sick. Of course, no one would approve of that today. Outside were two outhouses that were quite a distance from the school. If you had the urge to go to the outhouse, you held up your hand and were excused. In the winter it was quite traumatic going to the outhouse because of the extreme cold. There wasn't much trouble with kids loitering out at the outhouse in the wintertime, but that wasn't so in the early fall and late spring.

When we arrived in Idaho I was in the sixth grade. There were about seven or eight of us in the top grades that year. If I remember right, there were four of us in my class and I think about four others—one eighth grader, one seventh grader, and two fifth graders, or something like that, and we had quite a time. Some of the kids would get a little out of hand and the teachers had the authority to do anything to keep discipline. The paddle was used quite often and that would straighten up the whole room for quite a while—there would be no fooling around then. However, there were three boys—a Matthew boy, Harold McAffee, and Gordon Olson, who got out of line one time. The teacher took them out into the hall, leaned them over the table, and really gave them a swatting with the paddle. They didn't resist a bit. That sure made Christians out of the smaller kids who were there.

A favorite trick in the winter was to make paper balls and, under the pretense of taking them to the wastepaper basket, open the stove and throw the balls in the fire. The teacher didn't pay much attention until .22-gauge bullets were put inside the balls before they were put in the stove. The first few times the teacher didn't know what was happening. But, when she figured out what was going on, she put a stop to it. Sometimes, the explosion was so violent that it would blow the stove door open. Because coal was burned all the time I think she blamed it on a problem with the coal. But, it didn't take her long to figure out what was going on.

Some of the kids, who had to work on the farm until into late October when harvest was done, started to school late. They came late every year and never did make it out of the eighth grade.

At recess and noon in the spring and fall we would play outside. In fact, they made us go outside. There were just about enough kids in school that we could choose sides and play baseball and other games. I remember a ballgame when a gal named Ivy played—she was sure a clown. She couldn't hit the ball when she was up at bat. There was a left-handed kid that stood on the "other" side of the plate and, of course, batted left-handed. When she saw that, she thought that was the way to do it, because he would hit the ball every time. So she stood on the "other" side, the ball came through, and instead of batting it out to the pitcher, she went right on through with the bat and hit the catcher in the stomach. That doubled him up and took the fun out of baseball that day.

Only women teachers were hired back then. I never did have a man teacher until I went to high school. Because we lived in a very rural area (there was only a grocery store and a post office in Darlington) there was no place for a teacher to stay, except with a family. So Frigit Carlson's family, whose place was about a quarter-mile from the school, put them up quite often. They were related to us, of course. There were three Carlson kids. The oldest one was Orient and he was about Dad's age. Next was Marion, who was quite a bit younger, and then Eunice. Marion finally married one of the teachers who taught at Darlington.

In the winter it was quite a chore to get to school; it was so bitterly cold. Each year it would get down to 30 or 35 degrees below zero and the kids traveled quite a distance. They came by buggy before it snowed and was real cold. When the cold weather and snow came, they came in sleighs all bundled up. Some of them traveled six or seven miles. Most didn't have much for shoes, but their feet were wrapped in gunnysacks. It's a wonder kids survived those days. There was a family of Matthews that lived about five miles up the canal from the schoolhouse and they rode a horse. There were four of them and they would all four ride on that old white horse.

The summer of 1927 was work as usual. Except that the McAffees got a new Ford Roadster. It was still a Model T but in a color other than black. It was the first year that they put a door on the driver's side. Before, the driver had to get in the right side and slide over, or crawl over the side to get behind the wheel. We sure had fun driving on Sunday afternoons.

Life at Home

In August, things got more exciting. A buyer came and bought our lambs and I remember that we got a good price. Dad bought a second-hand Fordson tractor in Arco and I got to drive it home.[3] It stormed that day, so it was anything but pleasant.

An important event happened on the 13th of August that year—a baby girl was born. She was born at Darlington and named Edythe Geraldine Lindburg. She was premature by two months and was born at the Carlson's house because they had a couple of extra rooms. After two weeks she was brought home. She was sickly the first three months and we were fortunate she survived. There were no facilities to care for preemies like there are today. The only help she had was a special formula as a substitute for milk. Late one evening Mom discovered that she was out of formula. The only place it was available was a drugstore in Arco, which was about 16 miles from Darlington. It was about closing time so Mom had me go to Carlsons, who had the closest telephone, and call the drugstore to see if they would stay open until I could get there. They said they would. Dad was not home, so it was up to me to make the trip. All I had to drive was the old 1924 Model T Ford, with no top and no floorboards. It was a cold, moonlit night when the Model T and I took off for Arco. Today a trip like that would be routine, but not so in those days. The road followed the section lines so there were a lot of right-angled corners and no pavement. Part

---

[3] Roland was age 13 at this time.

was graveled, some was just dirt, but all was graded. I made the trip in record time, which pleased Mom, because Edythe had been crying all the time I had been gone. As soon as she had her bottle of formula she quieted right down. The four Lindburg boys were very proud to have a sister.

We needed firewood, so the next week or two we kept busy going to the mountains and hauling logs home with a team and wagon. As I remember, we made a trip every other day. Because we now had a tractor, Dad bought a buzz saw from Montgomery Ward that operated from the tractor by a belt, so we didn't have to saw the logs with a hand-powered crosscut saw. With the tractor and new saw we could cut the winter's wood in less than a day. It was a big improvement although it took two or three of us to run it, depending on the size of the logs.

My First Job Was at the School

It was the first week in September and time to start school. I applied for the job of janitor, and was interviewed by the school board. They thought I was capable so I got the job. The pay was $15 per month and I even started my own bank account. I was in the eighth grade and it meant I would spend a couple hours more at the schoolhouse each day. The job consisted of more than just sweeping and cleaning windows, blackboards, and so forth. The school was equipped with two coal-burning potbelly stoves, which meant carrying coal in from the coalhouse. When it was cold I would haul two buckets of coal for each stove. Because the drinking water was supplied by the well, I carried it by bucket into the hall so both rooms could use it. A dipper was supplied and hung on the side of the bucket. There was another bucket on the floor. If you wanted a drink you just dipped the dipper into the water and drank from the dipper. If you couldn't drink all that you took, you poured the remainder into the bucket that was on the floor. The teacher took the kids in the first grade to the water to show them how it was done. I believe they had a hard time reaching into the bucket that was on the table.

It took a lot of kindling to start the fires and the paper from the wastepaper baskets came in handy. That winter was cold and during the month of January it never got above zero. At night it would drop down to 30-below, so I would be sure to have the kindling and coal in the night before. There were only two of us in the sixth and seventh grades—just Jim McAffee and me. But when the Cobbleys moved back to Darlington there were five of us in the eighth grade. The Cobbleys had three children: Ralph and Roy were Mr. Cobbley's by his first wife, who had passed away; Maureen was Mrs. Cobbley's; and together they had a third family of about six kids. The next year they all moved to Challis.

Meanwhile, Back at the Ranch

The second cutting of hay was in the stack by the first of September. In the Lost River Valley, because of the elevation and short growing season, the grain was almost ready to cut. We used a machine that cut the grain and tied it in bundles. The machine was called a binder and it was pulled by three horses. The width of the cut was six feet. The first week of school, it was time to cut the barley. If we had no breakdowns it would take about 5 days to cut 80 acres. Dad ran the binder on Tuesday. On Wednesday I came home from school, after I got the janitor work done, and ran it until four o'clock. Dad spelled me while I went back to school and finished the janitor work. Dad ran it Thursday and finished the field on Friday. Next was the field of oats. It was only about 20 acres and Dad cut that.

Now, the grain had to be shocked (about six or eight bundles to the shock). That was done by setting them on end with the heads up so they would dry out. We had a hired man who did that. The first or second week of November, the grain was dry enough to thresh. It took about three bundle wagons to haul the bundles to the threshing machine—four would have been better. The wagons were regular hayracks pulled by horses, so it would take one man for each wagon and two men in the field to pitch bundles onto wagons. When the wagons were loaded, the driver would bring the load and feed the bundles into the threshing machine. It took one man to haul the grain away from the machine and shovel it into the granary. And, of course, it took one man to run the thresher. It took about three days to thresh all of our grain. A big shed, which was called a straw shed, was closed on three sides and opened to the south. When we threshed, the straw was blown on top and on the sides, making a warm place for the livestock. The barley went over 90-bushel to the acre. We kept what we needed to feed our livestock through the winter and sold the rest to a cattle feeder. We kept the oats for our horses because we fed them oats year-round. We had to grind the barley for the cattle and hogs. The sheep didn't need grain until lambing time. They could eat the whole kernel because they had good teeth.

All of the crops were in for the winter, except the spuds. They were dug the next two Saturdays when we kids were out of school. The only machine was a horse-drawn machine—sort of a plow that would go under the hill of spuds, raise them onto a wide chain, and drop them over the back onto the ground. Then they were picked by hand into sacks and hauled to the cellar.

We were in the process of remodeling our house at the time, but, when it appeared that winter was coming, Dad got some neighbors to help build two small buildings and connect them together. One was used as a kitchen, dining room, and bedroom for the folks. We four boys used the other as a bedroom. That winter was extremely cold, and it was a challenge to keep warm. Although the house we were remodeling had a new cement wall, it only had a dirt floor, so we kept things there that we didn't want to freeze. That was a lot of legwork running between the two houses and down to the basement to carry water from the well and wood in. And the outhouse was quite a distance from the living quarters.

I suppose you may not know what an outhouse is—so here is a brief description. An outhouse was a small building over a hole in the ground. It had a bench with two or more holes to sit on, which were carved in the shape of toilet seats. When the hole in the ground was full, another hole was dug and the building was moved over the new hole. It was important to fill the old hole with dirt. Some people built their outhouses over ditches, so when the water came down the ditch, the water washed the residue away and into the irrigated fields. We could always tell who those people were by the Sears and Roebuck Catalog pages all over their fields.

With winter approaching and the nights getting cold, the two buildings we were living in were very unsatisfactory, so it was decided to finish the basement of the house and live down there for a year. The three-room house I was born in was moved onto the north half of the basement, and had a covered stairway leading from the basement into the middle room of the house. A roof was built over the remainder of the basement. A stairway leading into the basement was built outside and enclosed. There were plenty of windows built through the concrete, and there was a large skylight over what was to become the kitchen, so we went to work to finish the basement. The walls were the most time consuming, as they had to be framed and lath had to be nailed on. After that, plaster was applied. My brother and I worked nailing lath after school and after chores were done. We had to do the inside walls on both sides. We worked into the night; we were in a hurry to get out of the cold that we were living in. To make a long story short, we moved in about a week before Christmas. A large state-of-the-art air-circulating heating stove from Montgomery Ward was installed. It was fired by wood. As it turned out, the basement was easy to heat and the registers that were installed in the floors of the bedrooms upstairs took the chill out of them.

The Holidays

A storm dropped about eight inches of wet snow before Christmas, so a team of horses and a sleigh was put to use, mostly to haul hay from stacks in the fields to the corrals. Dad did most of the hay hauling. On Saturdays, it was my job to grind barley for the hogs, milk cows, chickens, and the few turkeys we had. The setup that we had for grinding grain was a second-hand Burr grinder pulled by a Model T Ford engine that we had converted into a stationary engine. For a radiator, a 30-gallon barrel was used. It had hose outlets welded in it so the hoses could come from it to the engine. It sure put out a lot of steam in the cold weather.

Just before Christmas, a trip was made to Mackay to buy gifts. However, most of the gifts were from the Montgomery Ward catalog. How the folks got them from the post office without us kids finding out, I guess I'll never know. We went to the mountains and got our own tree—generally a very nice one. On Christmas Eve we exchanged gifts. During that time, Santa came (how he ever got down that stovepipe, I'll never know). Christmas Day we had a big dinner and it was all over.

Another big snowstorm left us with another ten inches of snow. We even had to use the team and sleigh to haul the milk to the cheese factory at Darlington and to get the mail. Christmas vacation was spent skiing on the butte on our place. Plenty of neighbor kids would come to ski there, too, so we had plenty of company. That Christmas I got my first store-bought skis. Before that, we had to make our own. Then came New Year's Eve—a cold, crisp, moonlit night where the frost sparkled like diamonds. We were about to witness one of the coldest Januarys on record. It would be more than thirty days before the thermometer would rise above the zero mark.

Winter of 1928

That bitter cold was the introduction to 1928. It meant more work, such as hauling hay, because the livestock needed more feed to keep warm. Grain had to be ground. And, the old Model T was the only vehicle we tried to run during cold weather. We heated water over a fire and poured it into the engine—then it would start. The engine that was used to pump water was started the same way. A special heater was used to keep the water in the stock tank from freezing. As there was no electricity in those days, it was fired by wood. It consisted of a kind of tunnel, extending from the side of the tank, down and along the bottom to the center. Then a long, round pipe, eight inches in diameter, extended from the main body of the heater vertically up through the water to about five feet in the air. If it was regularly tended to, it worked very well. Steam would rise above the water. The livestock loved it and drank a lot. A ten-gallon can and sleigh were used to carry water to the penned calves and to the hogs that were ready to farrow. We delivered the feed the same way. The hog house, where the brood sows were kept, was dug back into the butte that extended down into the barnyard. Dad and my brothers took care of the chores. I had my hands full with the janitor job at school.

Although I had warm clothes, I nearly froze before I arrived at the schoolhouse before sun-up. I got the fires built in record time, then pumped water and carried it into the schoolhouse. Because it would freeze if I left it in the hall, each room had its own bucket and dipper. The fires were going good and the rooms were warm when the kids started to arrive. It was too cold to ride horses so those who came from long distances used teams and sleighs. Some of the smaller kids' folks would bring them. The rest would walk. They were all well clothed. The teachers would arrive first and help the little ones get unbundled and then bundle them up after school. The teachers lived about a quarter-mile from school and they always walked. Sometimes in the afternoon, I would get my work done and leave before they did. I think they didn't want to go out in the bitter cold. At that time of year, it was dark when I left. When I'd get home that basement house felt like a palace. It was warm and cozy.

In February, the weather began to warm up and by the end of the month some days were above freezing. The sheep began to lamb. About 18 small pens were built in the east end of the straw shed—just big enough for one ewe in each. After the ewe lambed, she was kept there until the lambs were two or three days old. That meant water and hay was carried to each pen every day. About half of the ewes had twins and there were several triplets; several lambs had to be bottle-fed. Once in a while, a ewe would lose a lamb and we would try to get her to adopt one of the triplets. Occasionally, we skinned the dead lamb and tied the hide on the lamb that we wanted the ewe to adopt. Sometimes it worked, sometimes it didn't. Lambing was a 24-hour job. When the kids got home from school, they spelled Dad off and that meant double duty. The cows had to be milked, too, when I got home. After supper, Geryl and I would stay with the sheep until ten or ten-thirty. Then Dad would take over. That year, we had 21 bum lambs (lambs without mothers).

Mom had the job of feeding and raising them. I don't think she lost any of them. As they got bigger, feeding them was quite a job; they all tried to be first—no manners at all. Lambing was practically over in 20 days, with a few stragglers after that. We had a lot more lambs than we had ewes.

Warmer weather came in March, although we didn't lose much snow. In April the snow began to go and by the first of May the snow was melting fast. Most of the nights were above freezing.

By the second week of May, school was out. We in grade school had to take a test that was administered by the county superintendent. She came to our school, gave the test, and took our test papers with her. We were notified a few days later of our score. We all passed and my elementary school days were over. It was May 1928.

The Busy Summer

The rest of May and June kept us very busy. In May, we plowed and planted the crops and sheared the sheep. In June, the irrigation started. Sugar beets were added to our list of crops. Dad leased 40 acres and we planted the beets; the Utah Idaho Sugar Company contracted them. They furnished the seed, and advanced money for the thinning and hoeing (which was all hand labor), and the harvesting, which was not until late fall.

In the later part of June, Dad took delivery of a brand new Model A Ford. I think it was the first in the Lost River Valley and the cost was $485. I went with him to Mackay to get it, measles and all. I felt sick, but I wouldn't miss an opportunity like this. Besides, someone had to drive the Model T home. The Model A was a radical change from the Model T. It was a stick

Roland at the wheel of the new Model A Ford

shift and the gas tank was in the cowl instead of under the seat. We didn't have to measure the gas with a stick anymore—it had a gas gauge. It also had an ammeter, temperature gauge, and a speedometer, which the Model T didn't have. And it had wire wheels, larger tires, and a spare wheel and tire. It was a blue, two-door sedan—a real classy outfit. Its top speed was 72 miles per hour but we never drove it over 50 miles per hour. It was not safe to drive faster than that on the roads we had in those days, although, in that year, a new highway the whole length of the valley was being built. But it would be another three or four years before it was paved.

High School in Arco

The rest of the summer went by with the usual jobs and chores. School in the fall was a new experience for me as I was going to high school. I chose to go to Arco because friends of mine, Roy Neal and his sister, Eva, were going there and they had rented an apartment that had two bedrooms, and a large kitchen and dining area combined. Another girl, Helen Linderman, (a freshman like me) would room with Eva and I would room with Roy. We had the apartment because it was 16 miles to Arco from Darlington, so it wasn't practical to travel every day to school. Today, school buses run from Darlington to both Arco and Mackay, hauling both grade school and high school students. Darlington is on the county line between Butte and Custer Counties, so the kids around Darlington live in two different districts. Arco is the county seat of Butte County and Mackay is in Custer County. There used to be a school in Moore, which is about half way between Darlington and Arco, but all of those kids are now bussed to Arco.

The apartment's landlady and her husband occupied the other part of the house. She made us understand that there would be no hanky-panky, and she looked like she meant it. She was the dominate type and did the talking for herself and her husband, too. He was the manager at the Craters of the Moon National Monument, so he wasn't home much of the time.

High school was quite different from grade school but it didn't take long to learn the routine. One event that I remember was the Snipe Hunt. Now, Dad warned me about the Snipe Hunt, but I went along like it was new to me. At night, two of the sophomores would take one freshman boy (me) up on the hill north of Arco. They also took a gunnysack, a stick, and a piece of string. We built a fire, positioned the gunnysack downhill from the fire, and propped the sack open with the stick that had the piece of string tied to it. The idea was that the fire would attract the Snipe and he would run into the bag. I was supposed to jerk the string so the bag would close, trapping the Snipe, and then bring the bag down to the schoolhouse. But, after I was left alone in the dark, I waited until I was sure they were gone, and then went home to the apartment and to bed. I later learned that my tormentors got worried, went back up the hill to check on me, and when they didn't find me, they worried the rest of the night. The next morning, when they saw me in school, they seemed relieved, and then got angry and vowed to get even with me—which they did during Initiation Week.

Initiation Week was the most miserable week of my life. The sophomores took it upon themselves to show the freshmen their ways of higher learning. They were bossy and used big paddles. The teachers let them get away with it—it was called "tradition." Most of the sophomores were reasonable but a few were very cruel and overbearing. They would give orders and if you didn't move fast enough they would swat you with wooden paddles. All week we had to dress in crazy costumes and parade in the halls. It was a long week. Finally, at noon on Friday, we freshmen were put in chairs, blindfolded, and lined up in the hall. We were then fed a spoonful of cod-liver oil with a piece of raw oyster. Many of us vomited. The sophomores wanted us to clean up the mess but the superintendent stepped in, sent the entire freshman class home, and ordered the sophomores to do the cleaning. Although some of the sophomores were not involved, the whole class had to do the cleanup and it caused a lot of friction within the sophomore class. Roy said that some of them got sick, which added to the problem, but they all had to stay until the mess was gone. Mr. Neal came to take us home to Darlington for the weekend and he asked where Roy and Eva were. Although we knew why they were late, Helen told him she thought they had extra work to do. We were four sick kids that went home to Darlington that weekend. If I ever felt like quitting school, that day was it. I was told that was the last initiation that was allowed at Arco High School.

That was the first year that Arco had a football team but, because there were no other teams in the district, they had to play teams from out of the district, such as Hailey and teams in the Snake River area. So, they didn't have many games. I did not turn out for football. I had to be home in Darlington on Saturdays when they played their games, and I don't remember seeing them play.

I did turn out for basketball. There was an organized freshman basketball team, and I made the first string as a starting guard. And, because no other schools in our district had freshman teams, we had to play schools from out of the district. We played Hailey, Carey and Moreland, and the Gooding School for the Deaf sent a team. Playing them was weird because they couldn't talk, but they sure could play basketball. They were very loud. I was told that was because they couldn't hear themselves. That was a very rough game and we lost. It was our only loss. Another event that I remember was a freshman trip to the Heise Hot Springs swimming pool, which was located about 70 miles northeast of Arco on Birch Creek. The reason that stands out in my mind is that Dad let me take the new Model A Ford with a load of kids. The kids that rode with me were very good kids. They hardly made noise on the way up or back. Sometime after that trip I began to wonder if they were just good kids or terrified of my driving. Anyway, everyone had a good time.

In the fall of 1928, Herbert Hoover was running for President against Warren Harding, the incumbent. As it turned out, Hoover won. I remember wearing a lot of his buttons.

School's Out, Back to Work

In May of 1929, school was out and I was back in Darlington for another summer of work. We all pitched in to get it done. My job was plowing, and for that I used the Ford tractor. It was equipped with a two-bottom plow, which hung right on the tractor. It had a lever that I had to reach to pull the plow out of the ground. It was all I could do to lift it. It also pulled a section of harrow to break up the newly plowed ground. It took a long day to plow four-and-a-half acres. As I plowed, Dad would run the leveler. Four horses pulled it. It took me four days to plow what he could level in one day. Sometimes Geryl would do the leveling. That spring was cold and blustery so it was hard to keep warm on the tractor or the leveler. Sometimes there were snow flurries or a cold wind and it was just plain miserable.

We only worked six days a week, except for feeding livestock, milking cows and changing water. Other than that, we always went to Sunday school. Sunday school was held in a little cabin on Carlsons' land, which was just across the road from Darlington. It was equipped with wooden benches and had an old pump organ. Ruth Carlson (Orient's wife) was a very good musician and sure could make music on that old organ. We would sing the old hymns with gusto. I think there were about 15 people attending Sunday school regularly. The rest of Sunday we had to ourselves to do as we pleased, as long as we stayed out of trouble and were home to help with chores. The Lindburgs learned to be home on time at a very early age.

There was no church service in Darlington, except Mormon, because there was no minister. I would guess that about 80 percent of the population in the Lost River Valley was Mormon. There were several Mormon churches in the valley, including one at Darlington. The Darlington church had quite a large congregation and there was something going on there several times a week. It was a brick building with a full basement. The Post Office was just across the road from the log cabin where we held Sunday school and the people that ran it were named Rice. Mrs. Rice claimed to be the 53rd child of Brigham Young, of Mormon fame.

By the middle of June the crops were planted, the sheep sheared, and we settled down to keep all of the crops watered. In about two weeks we would be haying.

Lamb Cheese Company

As I mentioned before, Darlington had a cheese factory, which was owned by the Lamb Cheese Company. All of the farmers in the area brought milk to the factory and they were paid every two weeks. I delivered our milk most of the time. About that time, a group of farmers up Antelope Creek asked if I would haul their milk for them because I had made a pickup out of the old Model T Ford. I took the back seat off and built a wooden platform in its place. I could haul about 12 cans of milk. They offered me 15 cents a can, which would more than buy the gas and oil. I averaged about 10 cans a day, 7 days a week. That cut me out of Sunday school sometimes, although I got home early enough most of the time to get ready to go.

The cheese maker at the factory was a young fellow named Archie Baird who came to Darlington from Ririe, Idaho. At that time, Ririe was quite the dairy country. Archie learned to make cheese there at a large cheese factory. Archie had other interests and one of them was a young lady named Vera McAffee. He spent as much time as he could with her. One day Archie asked me if I would come late afternoons and help him clean up. After talking it over with Dad, we decided that I could do that. The pay was 50 cents an afternoon.

There was no electricity in Darlington in those days, so a steam boiler was required to furnish steam for the engines as well as the vats that held the milk. Several pulleys were spaced to power them and other machines in the factory. The vats were made of wood with metal linings and the milk was heated by opening a valve to circulate steam between the wood frame and the liner. Thermometers floated in the milk so we could tell when the milk was warm enough.

I learned the cleanup procedure without a problem. The only thing I was leery of was the boiler. The fire would have to be banked for the night. And, I had to see that it was full of water. The water came from a well inside the building by using a high-pressure pump pulled by a belt from the line shaft to a pulley on the pump jack. The water was stored in a 1,000-gallon tank over the coal bin and piped to places where water was needed. It was a little tricky getting the water in the boiler. A pipe with cold water and one with steam went into the injector, which pulled the water in. How you could force water into a boiler, against 100 pounds of pressure, I could never figure out. But, if you adjusted the injector just right, water would start into the boiler. There was a water glass so you could see how much water was in the boiler. I kept a close eye on the water glass because if the boiler ran out of water, it would blow a plug out of the bottom into the fire box and spread ashes all over the place. Then the boiler would be out of commission for days.

As time went by, Archie asked me to come earlier each afternoon to help him. Then he wanted me to stay after I delivered our milk. One day he showed me how to make the cheese, and soon after asked me to come before the farmers brought their milk in, so I could learn to weigh-in the milk and take samples to determine the butterfat. It was important to do that right because the farmer was paid on the amount of butterfat in his milk. I was learning all of the "ifs and ands" of making cheese.

School had started in the fall of 1929, but I had made up my mind that I was going to be a cheese maker and I wouldn't need any more school. My pay had increased to a dollar a day, which wasn't bad in those times. I didn't know that Archie was planning to get married and needed all the help he could get. Some days he would ask me to come early as he wouldn't be there until noon, so I would start the process. Sometimes we both would be there in the morning and he would be gone in the afternoon. As much as you might want to, you can't hurry the process of cheese making.

I had a hunch that Archie and Vera were going to get married, and my hunch was right. About a week later Archie informed me that he would be gone for three or four days and that he was confident that I could run the factory. There was no doubt in my mind. Archie also told me that if anyone asked where he was, that I should tell him that he wasn't feeling well. The four days went by without any problems. When Archie returned he plugged each cheese I had made (checking for texture or acidity) and they passed the test. I was convinced more than ever that I was going to be a cheese maker. Days went by. Some days I was there alone; some days we were both there; some days I was off.

Then one night the factory burned down. My cheese-making career ended right there. The loss of the cheese factory, to say the least, was a catastrophe for the farmers whose milk was going there. Some of them didn't know of the fire until they arrived with their milk the next morning. Archie was there and had already called the Lamb Company, which owned the factory. They told him to stand by and they would contact Kraft Cheese Company to see if they could take the milk. Standing by meant to stay by the only telephone, which was in a store at Darlington. It was a modern telephone that hung on the wall and needed to be hand cranked to call out. When the news came about noon, we learned that Kraft would take the milk at their Arco plant, which was 16 miles from Darlington. A representative from the company was in Darlington at 2:30 p.m. that afternoon at the Mormon Church. Many farmers agreed to send their milk permanently to Arco. Archie Baird was there and was asked to transport the milk. He declined but suggested that I might be interested in hauling it regularly. Dad was there and we decided to take on the job.

The Beginning of Lindburg Truck Line

We learned that there were 6 cans more than we could get on our old Model T truck, so we built a platform and made a second deck that would hold 8 cans. I made the first trip and found 29 cans were too heavy for the old Model T. Dad met me in Arco and made a deal with Fred Rich, the Chevrolet dealer, on a bigger truck. It was a used 1929 Chevy truck that was supposed to haul 40 cans of milk. That was a year before trucks had dual wheels.

Things went well with the milk route except that the old truck was overloaded. Because of that I installed new front bearings almost every afternoon. Because more farmers wanted to ship milk we were getting more milk than our truck would handle. So, the next step was to pull a trailer. The trailer was a chassis of an old car with the body removed and a wooden bed built on the frame and running gear. The bed was 2 cans wide and about 9 cans long. A tongue was fastened to the front axle with a steering mechanism attached to the tie rod. Now the trailer could be steered. We installed a short tongue so we could pull it behind a truck. (Later these were called Hoover wagons, because of the Depression.) Some of the wagons had long tongues so a team of horses could pull them. All had rubber tires so the ride was smooth, unlike the lumber wagon, which they replaced. Almost everyone made them.

We picked up milk with the old Model T, as well as with the Chevy. We then loaded all of the milk on the Chevy and trailer at Darlington and went from Darlington to Arco with the entire load. It was slow but we made do for a couple of months. This was the start of the Lindburg Truck Line. 1929 was passing by.

1929 will also be remembered for the crash on Wall Street and the start of the worst economic depression the United States has ever experienced. Herbert Hoover, who was President, was blamed, although he submitted many remedies to the Democratic Congress. They turned down most of them and things seemed to get worse.

School in Mackay

The milk route was well established and it was decided that I should go back to school. Dad decided that he could handle the route after the farm work was done, which was about the first week of October. His crew was the rest of the family, the hired man, and me, after I got back from the milk route. So, I went back to school. Starting a month late, we decided I would go to Mackay. Mackay was about 15 miles from home, so I would have to find a place to stay during the week, then go home on the weekends. I registered on the first day of school but didn't attend until the first of October. Geryl was a freshman that year and he also started a month late. But, we weren't alone. Several of the other farm kids were doing the same thing.

Geryl stayed at the Jim Pence home; they boarded several high school kids and charged 15 dollars a month. They promised that I would be the first on their list if someone would happen to drop out, but by the first of October, no one had. Dad was acquainted with a man named "Mac" Mackenzie. He owned a lot of corrals and bunkhouses, a big house, and several outbuildings, including two large barns adjacent to the railroad stockyards. He catered to stockmen, cowboys, or sheepherders and their horses during the big cattle drives. He also owned a restaurant uptown that was run by his daughter and her husband, whose names were Lafe and Maxine West. Mr. Mackenzie agreed to let me stay there and do a few odd jobs around the place for my room and board. As it turned out, he never found any odd jobs. There were several beds in a big room upstairs. I occupied one of the beds and I ate my meals uptown at the restaurant. After all, it was his restaurant.

I settled in one weekend and on Monday left for school, which was across town. As I approached the school grounds, a kid I had never met before came clear across the street to meet me and welcome me to school. He showed me all around and introduced me to some of his friends and to the teachers. The high school only had four teachers so they had to teach more than one subject. The basketball coach taught all of the history classes in the school.

I was a sophomore that year so it was mandatory that I take English, algebra, history and biology. Mackay had no football team in those days but they offered basketball, baseball, and track. They had an outdoor tennis court, but it wasn't a school-sanctioned sport. That was the first year that Mackay had a school band. I started in the band with an old cornet of Dad's that he played in the town band in Polk, Nebraska. The band teacher's name was Fritz Westenfelt who was a bandmaster in the Marines in World War I. Because he was a retired Marine, he served the school district without pay the first couple of years. He did most of his own music arranging for the different instruments. The year after I graduated, Mackay had an Idaho State Champion Band. (I might add that Helene Tschanz, my future wife, and my brother, Geryl, played in that band.) Mr. Westenfelt even organized a school orchestra, as well as a dance orchestra in which I played second trumpet. I also sang in the Glee Club that put on the operetta. During my school career I also played on the first string basketball team. That about sums up my activities during my sophomore year in school.

Trucking Picks Up

The milk route kept growing because the price of other farm products was low, but the milk price didn't drop much. It was the only steady cash that the farmer could count on. So, as more milk was produced, it was up to the Lindburgs to find a way to get it to the cheese factory. It was a challenge during January because of the snow and cold weather. We even used horses and a sleigh to pick up milk, and to start the trucks. It was a year or two before Prestone (antifreeze) was available, so we drained the radiators every night and refilled them every morning, most often with water heated on the kitchen stove. If there was no hot water available we relied on a gallon can filled with sawdust that was soaked with diesel fuel or kerosene. That was lit and set under the engines to warm them up. We then covered the radiator so that when water was poured in, it wouldn't freeze before the engine could warm up. In extremely cold weather we covered about half of the radiator with cardboard to keep it from freezing while we were running.

As the weather began to warm up we were getting more milk to haul, so we bought a 1930 long-wheel-base Ford truck with dual tires. That was the first year that size of truck was available. The tires carried 85 pounds of pressure (a high-pressure type). It could handle a fourteen-foot bed that was eight feet wide and had an upper deck that was seven feet long. It handled the milk without any problems. The milk was hauled in ten-gallon cans and we were paid 20 cents per 100 pounds of milk, every two weeks. As I remember, it amounted to about 200 dollars each check. Kraft Cheese Company wrote the check.

Word spread that we had trucks and were looking for commodities to haul. Because some farmers were looking for markets for their grain, and some cattlemen on the East Fork of the Salmon River were looking for supplement feed for their stock, there was a ready-made hauling job. The problem was getting them together. Dad solved it by buying grain from the farmers, and hauling and selling it to the stockmen, both cattle and sheep men. That worked well until the stock was taken to the range in the spring. That lead to the offer to haul cattle and sheep, and we needed another truck. The bank in Blackfoot had just repossessed a practically new Ford Model B. It had four cylinders, 50 HP, long-wheel-base with dual tires, and had a factory-built bed that easily converted to haul milk. A stock rack was built on the 1930 Ford.

The first stock we hauled was lambs for Alex Boyle, from about five miles above Clayton to the stockyards in Mackay. He had several hundred head, so we had to get another trucker to help us. His last name was Thurston and he was a milk hauler from Arco. He would make one trip a day after his milk run, which made a long day for him. About his third trip, he tipped a load over—into the river. The roads in those days were very narrow with turnouts every so often for oncoming cars. So, if you were close to a turnout and you saw a car coming, you just pulled into it and waited for the car to pass.

Mr. Mackenzie

I didn't realize it then, but the Mackenzie that I stayed with was the same Mackenzie that owned the saloon in Custer, when Custer was booming in the early 1900s. He also owned the livery stable and a barbershop. He had the contract to furnish wood for the boilers that made steam for the engines that ran the ore mill and the compressors that furnished air for the mining operations. He had the finest house in Custer, which has been restored and is a tourist attraction. When the mines at Custer shut down in 1909, he bought the property in Mackay where I stayed. Although he talked about the early days in Custer, I didn't know that he was Mr. Big. He never talked about his wife. I knew he had one because he had two grown kids, Maxine and Claude. Both "tipped the bottle." Claude stayed at his Dad's place in the same upstairs room where I stayed. He would come in anytime of the night drunk, and some nights not at all. It kind of interfered with my rest. Once, about the second week I was there, the cattle were coming in off the range to be shipped out to the feeders. They were kept in Mackenzie's corrals and facilities until most of the cattle were in. Then buyers would deal with the owners and the cattle were moved to the railroad stockyards to be loaded and shipped out. Mackenzie would furnish feed for the cattle while they were in his corrals, board the cowboys' horses in his barns, and had bunk houses where the cowboys could shower and clean up. Mackay had a JC Penney store at that time where the cowboys would buy whole sets of clothes and then go out on the town. And "go out on the town" they did. Although it was during prohibition and alcohol beverages were illegal, Lost River had a lot of bootleggers and stills. These cowboys knew where they could find whiskey if they wanted it. They would pick fights with the local boys and some would be thrown in jail. Some would spend their time and money gambling (which was legal then) and end up broke. Then they would be fighting mad, drift back to the bunkhouse, and raise a ruckus all night. I guess that after being out on the range with cattle all summer, they had a right to celebrate. After all of that, they would work cattle the next morning until the cattle were shipped out. Then they left and went back to where they were employed and wouldn't return until the next fall.

A Good Move

There was so much going on at the Mackenzies that I was glad when the Pences notified me that two of their boarders failed to show up, so I moved over to their place. It was handy to live across the street from school and handier to practice basketball from seven to nine o'clock each evening. There were four of us steady boarders staying at Pence's.

The Pence family owned a ranch where the Mackay Dam is now. When the dam was built in 1914, they were bought out and moved to Mackay. They bought a residence, meat market, and a slaughterhouse. There were six grown children in the family, two girls and four boys. Charley and Tom ran the meat market and slaughterhouse. Glen managed the lumberyard. One of the girls married a fellow from Firth, Idaho. The other girl married a local man named Leo Ivie, a very colorful and likeable guy. Jim, the youngest, was in school in Ohio. I don't believe he ever came back to Mackay. Tom was the only one living at home. He later married Eva Neal, who I boarded with at Arco.

Mrs. Pence tried to be strict and fed us well. She would try to keep track of our grades and was interested in all of our activities. I don't remember her ever leaving home but she seemed to know all of the latest news. She talked like she disliked most everyone in town.

Before I knew it, it was Christmas vacation. The Depression was just beginning to be felt in Idaho. The farmers felt it first when the price paid for livestock and commodities dropped sharply. The farmer that had to buy feed had to sell out, and jobs were getting scarce. Milk prices held up well, so everyone who could milked cows, and the milk route was doing very well.

40

The House Fire

This was the first Christmas I can remember when there was no snow on the ground. The Lindburg family had a very nice, big dinner as usual. But the day after, on December 26, disaster struck. Late afternoon, a fire burned the house down and everything in it was lost. We had just returned from the milk route. My three brothers were starting to do chores and Dad was getting a load of barley to take to cattlemen on the East Fork of the Salmon River the next day. So, we were lucky to be dressed in our warm winter clothes. Mom and Edythe weren't so lucky—they were in the house, and escaped with just what they were wearing. Orient Carlson took them to his place where everyone, except Geryl and I, stayed. We stayed with the Olsons, who were neighbors. People were very quick to help us. Nearly everything that was needed to start housekeeping, as well as clothes, was given to us. Dad forgot that he had bought insurance until the agent came with an adjuster to assess the damage. He found that he had coverage for 1,000 dollars, which was a lot of money in those days. That money bought stoves and other things that we needed. There was a large vacant house, about a mile from our place that we moved into. It was dirty and it looked like an impossible cleaning job. After the stoves were installed, the neighbors came with mops and brooms, and in two days, it was spick and span.

It was a large old house with six bedrooms upstairs, one bedroom downstairs, a large kitchen, a bathroom with no fixtures, three other large rooms downstairs, and a large front porch. It had no well, so we hauled water. The other drawback was that the toilet was 150 feet from the back door of the house, and on cold winter nights it was very inconvenient, to say the least. I didn't get in on much of the cleanup or moving because I was on the milk route most of the time. We moved in a few days after New Year. We were back in high school and, on weekends, we went home to help with chores and get settled in our new home. Because we had quite a lot of wool at the Logan Woolen Mill, they provided us with warm blankets and heavy clothes.

Back to Business

I would run the milk route so Dad could tend to the other trucking jobs, because that part of the business was building up fast. Some Sundays he would take a load of cattle to the stockyards in Ogden, Utah, so the cattle would be there for the Monday morning market, and he would return on Monday. On those Mondays I missed school to do the milk route. I did satisfactory work in school, and was good enough to make the traveling basketball squad, which had just eight players. Some of the town folks would volunteer their private cars to take us to out-of-town games. Traveling didn't interfere with other activities, except when we played Salmon City, which was 120 miles from Mackay. We stayed there overnight. On Saturday afternoon we played Leadore, which was 25 miles up the Lemhi River from Salmon, and traveled back to Mackay that evening.

The following summer was very busy. The shearing crew had just finished shearing the sheep when I got out of school. I ran the milk route, which had expanded from Leslie, five miles north of Darlington, to eight miles south of Darlington. So I crisscrossed the valley, visiting all of the farms that shipped milk. We generally tried to use two trucks and meet at Darlington, where we loaded all of the milk cans onto the larger truck. Then that truck would pick up milk to the end of the route and go on to Arco, arriving about 10:30 a.m. Any later than that would risk souring the milk (sour milk can't be used to make cheese, so any sour milk was always sent back to the farmer).

Whey is a waste product of cheese making and a good liquid feed for hogs. The dairy farmers who were also growing hogs would have first chance to have their cans returned full of whey, which was pumped out of the factory to an elevated tank. We drove along side of the tank, opened a valve, and placed the hose in the can to fill it. Even so, that was extra work for the route driver. The cheese maker at the Kraft Plant was Oscar Johnson. He owned a small ice cream freezer and often made ice cream. So, when the milk was unloaded and the whey was loaded, we would be treated to a dish of ice cream before we started home.

A Little Geography

The following is a little about the geography of the Big and Little Lost Rivers of Idaho where I spent my boyhood. There were six settlements in the Big Lost River Valley, starting upstream: Chilly, Mackay, Leslie, Darlington, Moore, and then Arco at the lower end. The head of the Big Lost River starts on Trail Creek Summit; on the other side of the summit, Trail Creek runs through Sun Valley and empties into the Wood River. As the river runs down the valley, several creeks join it; a large stream comes out of Copper Basin. It then flows through several ranches that use water from the river for irrigation, and continues toward Chilly. There it sinks—and is referred to as the "Chilly Sinks." The riverbed is dry then for about five miles. It appears again and goes north toward Willow Creek Summit. There are a lot of wetlands, sloughs, meadows, and such that contribute to the flow of the river. After running through several more ranches, it joins a large stream before reaching the Mackay Dam. Nearly all of the canyons on both sides of the valley have water in them, but very few of them ever reach the river except during the spring runoff. The dam stores the water so the farmers down the valley have water all summer. The river then flows down the valley until it gets below Darlington. It sinks again and is a dry bed until it gets just below Arco. There it reappears and runs out onto the Arco Desert, where it sinks for the last time. That's why it's called Lost River.

The Little Lost River is east of the Big Lost River, just over the mountain range known as the Lost River Mountains, which is the highest range in Idaho. The Little Lost River gets it starts at the summit, between the summit and the Pahsimeroi River, which flows north and empties into the Salmon River. The Little Lost River flows south until it gets to Howe and then it sinks into the desert. Geologists claim the two rivers came together under the lava flow that covered the area several thousand years ago as the result of an eruption of the Craters of the Moon. It flows more than 100 miles under the lava and then emerges as Thousand Springs on the Snake River west of Twin Falls, Idaho. The water gushes out of the cliffs above the Snake River and Idaho Power has a large power plant there.

The Drought

In 1931, the Lost River Valley was beginning to feel the drought and irrigation water was in short supply because of lack of snow in the high country. Utah Construction Company had a big reclamation project west of Arco and claimed first right to the water because they built the Mackay Dam, which is located above Mackay. The dam was built in 1914 and we were one of the few farmers in the valley who had an older right than that—one established in 1879 for 80 acres. The rest of our ranch had a later right, and because there was not enough water, we let some of our place dry up. Because of that and low crop prices, most of our attention was on trucking.

The drought was a major concern for the people of the Big and Little Lost River valleys. The Big Lost River was very lush, with an abundance of vegetation such as cottonwood and willow trees and underbrush of wild currants and gooseberries, which made good forage for cattle and other livestock. There were a lot of sloughs in the valley and some of them were large enough to support an abundance of fish. It was easy to see the fish because the water was so clear. Little steams would connect the sloughs so the water was always fresh and pure. John McAffee said that when he moved to the valley, east of Darlington, in the early 1900s, he had no well for water. So, he would carry water in a bucket from the sloughs. He said that he sometimes dipped up a fish. Sounded kind a fishy, but knowing John, I believe him (he wasn't one to tell any tall tales). The drought killed all of the lush growth along the river from Leslie, which is five miles above Darlington, all the way past Arco. Even the river at Darlington had very little water in it. To save what water there was in the river, the U.S. Reclamation Service used bulldozers and took all of the bends out of it—in other words, they straightened the river and made a canal out of it. I think that kept the river from coming back like it was before the drought.

The farmers who were losing their water were blaming the Utah Construction Company for taking more than half of the water for their farming project on the desert west of Arco. They built a canal that was more than 20 miles long and started about four miles above Darlington. Some of the farmers took the law into their own hands and attempted to blow up the Mackay Dam. They didn't hurt the dam much, but they did damage the control gates. The gate was blown open so the water was draining out of the dam. They also blew out the diversion dam that was built in the river to divert the water into the Utah Construction canal. No one seemed to know who did it. The sheriff did a lot of snooping around and believed a Chevrolet truck like ours was used and came down to question us a couple of times.

No one was ever convicted or even arrested. After that, Reclamation took over regulating the water in the valley and the Utah Construction Company was out.

Because of the drought, the government was lending money to the farmers—who could prove need—to buy feed to save their livestock. So, we hauled a lot of feed. Also, the state was building a new road from Mackay to the dam using horses and Freezenolls[4] so we hauled a lot of hay for the horses. The hay was handled with pitchforks because there was no baled hay around in those days. The summer of '31 was about gone and it was time to start school again.

Tales of School

I went to school the first week and then I missed the next two weeks, and went intermittently for a while after that. I wasn't alone—Geryl missed a lot of school as well. Hilmer was eleven years old and very big and strong for his age. He was still in grade school, so he was a lot of help in the mornings and evenings. Mornings and evenings Dad ran the milk route and then worked into the night hauling feed so we could go to school. We missed an occasional day to help him out and, of course, we worked weekends. I was a junior that year and my subjects were History, Physics, English, and Geometry. Geometry was difficult for me because I missed so much school when the fundamentals were taught. However, I worked hard and managed to pass. The other courses I managed well. I also took Band and Glee Club and played basketball. All of that kept me busy.

---

[4] Fresno scrapers, commonly known as fresnoes

We had a new basketball coach (his name was Bennett but I can't remember his first name). He made sure that we understood that it took discipline to be a good basketball team. Anyone who didn't obey the rules would not be on the team, and that person's uniform would be turned in. I remember he wanted us to be home by eight p.m. and to get a good night's sleep before a ball game. He also asked us to eat at four o'clock the day of the game, preferably a beef steak for protein, and no smoking. He caught two kids smoking and their uniforms were turned in the next day. I decided not to tell Mrs. Pence about the meal on the day of the game because she might raise my board. But, she found out about that and she informed me that I was to be there right after school because my beef steak dinner would be ready. She also found out about the rest of the rules and tried to enforce them the best she could.

A couple that graduated the year before had just gotten married and a party was held for them on the night before a game. The coach told us not to attend and said he would check to see if any of us were there. If he caught us there, we would be off the team. Joe Ausich didn't think the coach would go because he had only been in Mackay a short time and didn't know the recently married couple. So, Joe attended the party. He felt a little uneasy and asked his friends to be on the lookout for the coach. When they told him the coach was coming, Joe rushed into the bedroom and got under the bed. The coach stayed a while and then left. When told the coast was clear, Joe opened the bedroom window, crawled out, and took off for home. As he crossed the yard he ran right into the coach. "Where ya going, Joe?" The reply was "Home." That was the end of Joe's basketball career at Mackay High.

Helene's brother, Otto Tschanz Jr., was in the school play that year and his part required him to carry a suitcase when he entered the scene. During practice he always forgot the suitcase. The night the play was performed for the public, Otto entered without the suitcase, confusing the cast. Otto looked around a bit and then realized the suitcase was missing and exclaimed, "I forgot that darn suitcase." I guess that was the highlight of the performance. Otto was only a freshman that year. And, although Helene was still in grade school, she was the piano player for all of the musical groups such as the Glee Club and high school orchestra. She also played trumpet in the band and pep band. Christmas was around the corner and then all of the Christmas performances were over. We were dismissed for Christmas vacation. The year of 1931 was just about over.

There were no major snowstorms that year. On New Year's Eve it clouded up and looked as though a good storm was coming, but only a few flakes fell and so the drought continued. We were back in school the first Monday after New Year's Day. January was cold and dry and nothing out of the ordinary happened in school.

The Family Toils On

The demand on the trucking business was growing and we needed another truck. Someone had ordered a 1932 Ford but was unable to take delivery so we acquired that truck at a reduced price, financed at the Butte County Bank in Arco. It had a 50-horsepower engine, long wheelbase, a four-speed transmission, and a factory bed with stake sides. We modified it with another deck so it could be used on the milk route. The upper deck could be removed easily if need be so the truck could be used for other purposes. The biggest demand was hauling cattle and sheep. We also hauled quite a few hogs.

Hilmer was now about twelve years old and handled those ten-gallon cans of milk without any problem. And he was a good truck driver. No driver's license was required in Idaho at that time. Hilmer would pick up the milk between Darlington north to Leslie, crisscrossing the valley while Dad did the farm chores. Then Dad would take over and finish loading the milk south of Darlington on to the end of the route and into Arco. All shippers were required to have two sets of cans, so we left the empties when the full ones were picked up. The cans, which had a shipper's number painted on them, were furnished by Kraft at cost, which was deducted from the shipper's milk check. On weekends I would run the whole route while Dad and my brothers did the farming and delivered government feed to the farmers. We also had to grind grain and haul hay to feed our own stock for a week or more. Once in a while we missed a day of school to keep up.

It was February and things at school were going well and the basketball tournament was coming up. The tournament was always held in Mackay because we had the only gymnasium with a regulation basketball floor and room for spectators. We thought we had a good team but we came in third behind Challis and Salmon City. I played in each of those games and we had foul trouble.

In March, the school operetta was presented. We spent a lot of time practicing. I was the lead baritone. A girl named Leona Ivie was the lead soprano and we had a very good tenor—a kid named Dutch Hurst. The name of the operetta was "New Moon." We must have done a good job because we were asked to perform a second time.

In April we were practicing for a track meet that was held in Challis. It snowed two inches during the meet. I discovered that I wasn't much of a track star, as I couldn't place in any events that I entered.

The Sheep Industry

There were several thousand head of sheep in central Idaho in the 1920s and 1930s. Sheep were profitable because they produced two crops of lambs and wool each year. The owners of several large sheep operations in our area had grazing rights on the forest and Bureau of Land Management lands and they hired quite a few people to help them tend their flocks.

The sheep were grouped into bands of about 1,200 sheep each. Each band required a sheepherder and a camp tender and a couple of dogs, usually border collies. When they were out on the range they lived in covered wagons. When they were up in the mountains where wagons couldn't go, they lived in tents. The camp tender cooked all of the meals, did all of the chores around the camp, and moved the camp when it was necessary. The sheepherder and his dogs tended the sheep and brought them back to camp each night. Sometimes, if the sheep were grazing too far away from camp, the tender would move the camp to the sheep. If the owner had several bands, he would need someone to supply the camps with whatever was needed. Sometimes he would visit a camp and take the supply order and bring it on the next trip. In the winter, the sheep would be brought back to the ranch and fed hay and grain. If an owner had several bands, he would contract a farmer to grow feed for them and, in that case, the sheep would be moved to the feed.

We hauled feed for some of the sheep men, usually from the Snake River country where beans were grown. The sheep men would buy the cracked beans at the elevators that cleaned the beans. Sometimes they bought cottonseed pellets or corn that was shipped from out of state by the railcar load. We then would unload the feed from the railcar onto the truck and haul it to its destination.

In May, the sheep were brought down to the shearing corrals, which were usually on the range. The corrals needed to be where vehicles with the shearers' equipment could easily get in and the wool could be hauled out. Some of the sheep men asked us to haul their wool from wherever they sheared to the railhead at Mackay or Ketchum, and load it on railcars.

That was a little different from anything we had done before. The difference was the size and weight of the sacks of wool. A wool sack when it is full is eight feet long, two feet wide, and weighs about 200 pounds. We used no side racks on the trucks, just the flat beds and we loaded the sacks cross ways. That made our load the legal width allowed on the public roads. A load would be four sacks long on a twelve-foot truck bed and four sacks high, secured with rope and tighteners. During May and the first two weeks of June we kept one truck busy hauling wool, and often used the milk truck in the afternoons and evenings after that truck completed the milk route. The owner of the wool would supply a man to help load and unload. One person couldn't do it alone.

The wool was put in the sack with a rack that resembled the base of a windmill. It was about nine feet high with a platform on top. The woolsack hung down the inside of the platform. The top had a round hole the same diameter as the sack, with a steel ring that secured the sack at the top. As the sheep were sheared, a man would tie the wool from each sheep into a bundle and drop it into the sack. A person inside of the sack, referred to as a wool tramper, packed the wool. A good tramper would tramp the wool in the sack solid enough so the sack would be rigid. When two men lifted it, one on each end, it wouldn't sag in the middle and was easy to handle. Wool trampers, who claimed to be professionals, and the person who tied the pelts, and the shearers made up the crew that traveled and contracted to shear sheep.

In August, the lambs would be ready to go to market. We were hauling lambs to the railheads that formerly had been herded or driven to market. Trucks were taking over the old sheep and cattle drives. We loaded the lambs only. The ewes were left on the range and were spared the long drive to the railhead and back. It became apparent that we needed more trucks, but we made do that summer and fall by running what we had, and planned for next year.

To "make do" meant running the trucks 24 hours a day if necessary, and that required long hours of driving. When hauling lambs, I remember Dad would go 24 hours without stopping except for meals, mostly in restaurants in Mackay. Sometimes I would take the milk truck, move the cans to the raised platform that we built, and get a couple of my brothers to help take off the rack that we used to haul milk cans. We put on the stock rack with the double deck and off I'd go to haul lambs, trying to haul a couple of loads before I had to have the truck back for the milk route, which was usually not before daylight the following day. We'd change the racks, wash out the truck, and load the cans just in time for one of my brothers to start the milk route. Sometimes we would have to repeat the procedure for several days until we finished hauling lambs. The owners always had plenty of help to load the lambs when we got there, because they were hard to load and would never do what we wanted them to do. We usually had to pick them up and shove them into the truck. Occasionally, an owner had a goat to lead the sheep. It would go right up the chute, into the truck, and then it would work its way to the back of the truck. The owner would take him out and shut the tailgate, and we were loaded and on our way. It was a big relief to be finished hauling lambs.

The farm was being neglected because of the work for the trucks that was coming our way. Dad was planning to sell the sheep. Dutch was doing most of the work taking care of them and had to go back to school soon. We were still trying to take care of the grain and hay with the help of the hired man, but with the shortage of water and the prices of farm produce, the profits were not that great. Although we could sell the grain for feed to the sheep men through the truck line, the profits were still marginal. So, we concentrated on the trucks.

Autumn Again

September of 1932 was upon us and school was about to start. This would be my last year in school. Geryl and I moved back to the Pences. We were at school the first day to register. Then I had to go on the milk route because Dad was making a couple of trips to Ogden, Utah, with cattle. I missed about six days of school and went back until the first of October. Then it was back on the milk route while Dad threshed our grain. He also had to help the neighbors do their threshing to repay them for their help threshing ours. I was out of school about two-and-a-half weeks while Dad and the hired man did that and finished some of the fall work. On weekends we did chores such as dig potatoes, grind grain, etc. Catching up with my school-work was a little tough. This was the first year that they offered typing and it was one of the subjects that I chose. It wasn't too hard but took a lot of practice. Sometimes I would stay after school to practice. Another subject that I chose, that was new to me, was chemistry. It was interesting so I didn't have much trouble with it. I was really interested in the mercury that we had in the lab. We would snitch a little mercury and rub it on a penny. It would adhere to the copper and make it bright silver. Of course, it would rub off after we carried it around in our pockets for a few days. (This was before mercury became poisonous.) History was a cinch but English wasn't too interesting. Band, Glee Club, and basketball were my activities during my senior year. Our basketball team looked very promising and we had a good chance for the district championship that year.

Salmon River Merchants

I didn't miss many days of school during November and December. We made the most of the Thanksgiving holidays and weekends so Dad could make trips to the Salmon River with feed. He was going about once a week, mostly on Saturdays.

There was no freight service for the merchants on the upper Salmon. Their freight was routed to Challis and then sent up on the mail stage, which was a pickup with a homemade box or canopy. So, the merchants began sending orders with Dad to be filled at the wholesale houses when they learned he was going to Pocatello. To haul their gasoline, we acquired a 500-gallon portable tank that could be loaded and unloaded easily on a truck. Before we got the tank, all of the gas was delivered in 50-gallon barrels. It was a chore to get the barrels back to the shipper. We were using quite a lot of gas ourselves and had to get it in barrels. The Shell wholesale dealer in Arco installed an underground 500-gallon tank with a gas pump; the kind that had to be pumped by hand to a glass, 10-gallon tank that was about six feet above, and was equipped with a hose and nozzle. We filled our truck gas tanks with that. It sure beat getting the gas out of barrels into a gas can and pouring it into the truck tanks with a funnel.

With the increase in business, it became apparent that another truck was needed so we ordered a 1933 Dodge truck from a dealer in Blackfoot. They also financed through a finance company that they owned. It was to replace the old Chevy that was just worn out. At school, all of the Christmas programs had been rendered and we were out for Christmas vacation.

The Depression Deepens

The Depression was really being felt in the western states, especially in the Lost River country. With the drought, it was a double blow. Taxes couldn't be paid and the school districts were about broke, as were other taxing districts. The prices dropped even lower for livestock and other farm commodities. The storekeepers had been giving credit—so much that they were in trouble and had to go on a cash basis. For some reason, milk prices held up pretty well, so the milk route held up very well. Those milk-route checks every two weeks were our salvation. As payment for some of the other hauling jobs, we had to take meat or whatever else we could use, such as grain. We hauled it to the Salmon River and sold it. There was plenty of water in the river, so they didn't feel the drought like the Lost River country did. The Snake River, located to the south of Lost River across the Arco Desert, had plenty of water for the area's needs. Although the Depression hit the whole U.S., the freight trains of the Union Pacific were just loaded with men and their bedrolls. They were coming from the Midwest, where they were having a severe drought and high winds. It was known as the "Dust Bowl." These men were willing to work but couldn't find jobs. Huge soup kitchens were set up in the major cities to serve those who didn't have enough money to buy something to eat. Pocatello was one of the cities with a soup kitchen and also a main Union Pacific Railroad terminal. There were round-houses where the engines were repaired and also acres of switchyard. A lot of men tried to find work there, but the railroad could only use so many of them and the rest were turned away.

Otto's Ice Business

Shortly after school resumed, I was down in Hudd's Confectionery, the candy and ice cream store owned and run by

Otto Tschanz. He asked if we would be interested in hauling ice for him, starting the next week. I told him that I would check with Dad and let him know. As luck would have it, Dad was in town the next day and we decided we would haul the ice if I could stay out of school to do the hauling. I'll try to explain Otto Tschanz's ice business. Of course, those were the days before refrigerators. Households relied on iceboxes to keep food cold, so Otto was the man who delivered ice to all the houses and businesses that wanted or needed ice. He delivered the ice from an old Model T Ford that was converted into a pickup with a short 2-by-4 angled diagonally. A scale hung from the upper end. He sold ice by the pound. He got his ice by harvesting it from the Mackay Dam, located about five miles upriver from Mackay. He needed about 500 tons to supply the needs of Mackay. He stored the ice in a big warehouse in town. Each block of ice weighed 200 pounds, and an ice saw was used to make smaller pieces. The average household icebox held about 50 pounds. I'll refer to the warehouse as the "icehouse." The ice was packed in sawdust to keep the air from it and it would stay frozen all summer long.

The ice on the Mackay Dam freezes to about 3½ to 4 feet thick. Because of the water running into the lake in front of the dam, there is a bit of open water between the ice and the shore, and a bridge was required to get the trucks out on the ice to load. Otto had built a sled powered by a Model T Ford engine. It was pulled by hand over the ice and the saw blade would cut through 18 inches. Then the blade would be lifted and another cut made 18 inches from the first one, and so on. That made several cuts the same size parallel to each other. Of course, the 18-inch deep cut isn't much on ice 4 feet deep, so a tool called an ice spud was used. It was an iron bar 4 inches wide with a sharp point tapered up the bar about a foot and had a round handle about 4 feet long. It was used to strike the saw cut in the

Otto Tschanz and Mott Clark harvest ice on Mackay Dam

ice. The ice would break straight down, just as straight as if it had been sawed. A block, 18 inches by 18 inches by 4 feet would float out in the pond, ready to be loaded onto the trucks. The short end of a pole had a chain with ice tongs attached to it. The long end had a long rope tied to it. One man would hook the tongs to the block and then the other man would pull on the rope. They would lift the ice out of the pond onto the truck. Then the truck would drive toward the shore, across the bridge, and into town to the icehouse.

All of the sawdust from the previous year was removed from the icehouse except for four feet that was left on the floor for insulation. There was a long chute that reached the back of the truck when it was backed up to the door and it extended about half-way into the icehouse. We slid the blocks of ice to the back of the truck and onto the chute. The ice would slide into the icehouse where two men would place them in the center and no closer than four feet from the outside walls. As the pile of ice got higher than the truck bed, the blocks had to be pulled up onto the pile. That was done with a rope and pulley, which was attached to the side of the icehouse. The rope went through the pulley and was fastened to Otto's Model T ice wagon, which furnished the power to pull the ice up to the pile. The icehouse held 500 tons of ice. After the ice was packed in the center of the icehouse, it was one big block of ice. Then sawdust was packed around the ice and between the ice and the outside walls. Five feet of sawdust was put on top of the pile and the doors were closed. They would not be opened until the ice was needed the next summer.

Some unusual things happened at the pond during ice harvest season. Some years before, Otto had a Methodist minister with a Dodge truck haul ice for him. That was in the days before duel wheels and smaller trucks; 2½ tons was about the maximum haul weight. The Dodge was backed up to the pond. After it was loaded, the minister got the crank and went to the front of the truck. As he pulled up on the crank, the engine started. The truck was in reverse and it backed into the pond—into 30 feet of water. That left the minister holding the crank. It took ten days and a lot of hard work to raise the truck and get it up on the ice again.

When I first started hauling Otto's ice, I was driving from the road to the ice pond. It was a bright sunny day, but still about 30 degrees below zero. It was my first trip of the day—about eight o'clock. Mott Clark, Otto's helper, was operating the saw. I suppose Otto was breaking the ice that had frozen on the open water. Although Otto was there, I didn't see him. Just as I drove up I spotted him in the water, hanging onto the ice with both elbows. Mott Clark couldn't hear him hollering because of the noise of the saw. I honked my horn and Mott looked up. He saw Otto in the water, ran over, and jerked him out of the water. As soon as Otto was out of the water, his clothes froze stiff. He ran to his car, which was about 200 yards away on the shore, and took off for home. I didn't see Otto again until two o'clock that afternoon. I guess that wasn't too unusual. I was told he fell in nearly every winter. Maybe that contributed to his long life (99 years).

Then ice harvest was over and I was back in school and faced the task of catching up with my studies. I was able to go to basketball practice because we practiced in the evenings. I also got to play in a couple of games, so I really didn't miss any basketball. It was tournament time in about a week. The weather was warming up as the tournament started. We did very well until the last night; we played for the championship and had to settle for second place.

Financial Hardships

On January 20, 1933, Franklin D. Roosevelt was inaugurated as President of the United States. Shortly thereafter he took over the office. As president, he declared a bank holiday (which meant the bank could not pay any money out or accept any deposits). It was said that action was needed to stop a run on the banks because so many of them were going broke. The bank holiday was a hardship for many people. Otto Tschanz was one of them. He had money in the bank to pay for his ice harvest. Fortunately, the "holiday" only lasted for a week or two. Then we received payment for hauling ice.

The last week in February we learned that the school district had enough money to finish the school year, and that we were required to attend school on Saturdays for the next six weeks. Then school would be out for the rest of spring and summer. The teachers were to receive warrants but they weren't convertible to cash until they were called in. That would be when the district had the money to redeem them. The merchants agreed to accept them for groceries and cash, with the bank's help. I guess that satisfied the teachers. A little cooperation from everybody and we got by very well.

We learned that graduation would be April 9 for the class of 1933. It was tough for me especially in typing, as I had to type 30 words a minute without error to get a credit in typing. I felt I would have no trouble with the other subjects if I worked at them. But, I spent all of the time that I could practicing typing. We had no class pictures or class rings because so many of the kids couldn't afford them. Some of the boys knew that in every keg of horseshoe nails there were a lot of nails that were bent in a perfect circle. So they went to the hardware store and got enough so everyone in the class could have one. They didn't fit very well. Some of the girls wore them on a string around their necks. I wore mine on my thumb—it was in my pocket most of the time. My worries about graduating were for naught as I passed all of my subjects. When I went back for our 50th reunion I was really surprised to learn that some of my classmates did not graduate—they got blank diplomas. Some of them went to other schools to finish high school; others didn't go any further.

Graduation night was quite an affair. Ilene Murray was salutatorian; I don't remember who was valedictorian. Three of us were in the Glee Club that sang a couple of songs and the school orchestra played a couple of numbers. Four of us seniors played in the orchestra. Then back onto the stage to receive our diplomas. Immediately following, a dance was held in the gym and the orchestra played. We played until one o'clock, then everything was over but the shouting. My school days were over.

The Business Continues to Grow

After getting off of the milk route in the afternoons, I was responsible for the maintenance of the trucks. In Darlington, a fellow had built what was to be a service station but it was never finished. We used it and he helped to maintain the trucks. I learned a lot about trucks that was useful throughout my life. I spent most afternoons maintaining equipment.

We finally took delivery of the 1933 Dodge truck. Dad was busy building a flat bed and stock rack for hauling cattle, sheep, and hogs. Geryl and Dad were developing the general merchandise route for the merchants on the upper Salmon River and it was getting profitable. We had a visit from the Idaho State Public Utilities Commission, informing us that we needed a permit and were left a form to fill out. We had to list all of the towns that we intended to serve. So, we listed all of the places between Pocatello and home. We also included Hailey, Ketchum, May, Ellis, Salmon City, and Howe. We answered all of the other questions and sent it to Boise. To our surprise, we got everything we asked for, even some of the places we had never served. We were assigned the number 53 and we had to display the number on all of the trucks we used on that haul. Our agreement also called for a trip a week, or more if needed. A lot of the time the truck that was returning from Ogden, Utah, would stop in Pocatello and pick up the general freight and bring it to Darlington. There it would be transferred to another truck and Geryl would take it from there and deliver it to its destination. All of the people on the upper Salmon used our service and gave us tips of other businesses, such as some small mines that were starting up.

The Depression Worsens

The Depression was getting worse by the day, and the new president and his Democratic congress had a lot of ideas. They started the Works Progress Administration (WPA), designed to help the rural people who didn't have an income. The WPA required everything to be done by hand. Other than that, only wagons could be used. They were equipped with low beds for hauling gravel. So, a man and his team of horses would be hired to haul and help load the gravel. The gravel was used on the county roads. If the person didn't have a team and wagon, he would be hired to help load the wagons and spread the gravel. It was river-run, coarse gravel, and it made rough roads. But, at least the roads were never muddy. There was also a commodity program that furnished flour, beans, and other dry foods and, of course, there were the Civilian Conservation Corps (CCC) camps. The camps were located in the mountains, not too far from towns. There were two camps not too far from Mackay: one at Pass Creek and the other at Wild Horse. (The Devil's Bedstead resort is now on the site of the Wild Horse CCC camp.)

The county had a poor farm near Challis at the Challis Hot Springs that would accommodate folks who had no place to live and no funds to rent. They were furnished room and board. The ones who were able-bodied raised vegetables and other commodities to help support the farm. Because of the hot spring, there was a modern swimming pool. (We used to go there to swim once in a while. Because we were not residents, we had to pay to use the pool.) The county also had a relief program. Stores were given a list of people who were eligible. Recipients could receive only staples—no luxuries such as tobacco and candy. The stigma of being on relief was quite degrading in those days, so people on relief did their best to keep it a secret.

Dad used the new truck to haul a load of cattle to the Ogden stockyards. For a back-haul, he brought a load of salt that was coarse and quite wet. The shores of Great Salt Lake had several inches of salt that was suitable for livestock and wildlife. The farmers along the lake would go to the beach and, using horses and scrapers, would scrape the salt into piles and sack it in 50-pound bags. When the various cattle associations learned about the salt, we had all of the orders we could handle as back hauls. Also, the Idaho Game Department asked us to furnish salt for them.

It was about time to haul wool again and we acquired a couple of new customers. We loaded four or five railcars of wool that year. We took two small shipments right into Ogden. That suited us because we could always back-haul salt.

Dr. Phelps

This was the second year that we hauled wool for Dr. Phelps and he wanted us to haul his lambs from the range to a railhead. He also raised cattle that would be ready to ship in the fall. Dr. Phelps owned a large ranch in Round Valley on the Salmon River near Challis. His ranch consisted of bottomland near the river, a couple of miles before it leaves Round Valley and goes into a narrow canyon on its way toward Salmon City.

I think I'll use this paragraph to describe the life of Dr. Phelps as it was told to me and as I knew him at the ranch. He came to Custer as a young dentist in the 1890s while the Custer Mine and Mill was running full blast. While he was in Custer he married the daughter of the mine and mill superintendent. Her name was Ethyl Thompson. When the mine closed down and people were leaving Custer, Dr. Phelps took his practice and moved to Idaho Falls. While living in Idaho Falls, he was bitten by a deer fly that eventually left him paralyzed from the waist down. That was when he bought the ranch and developed it with sheep and cattle. The ranch produced a lot of alfalfa hay. He and Ethyl had three girls and a boy, who was quite lame. Dr. Phelps ran the ranch from the back of a horse. His old dentist chair and paraphernalia can be seen in the Custer Museum today.

It was becoming quite clear that we were getting more work than we could handle with the trucks and drivers we had. We decided we could get by until it was time to haul lambs. We now had two trucks with stock racks. One was the old 1930 Ford that was about worn out even with the second engine.

4th of July

It was the 4th of July and a rodeo was the main attraction that year. One of the events I'll always remember was the chair race. There were 11 chairs lined up on the racetrack and 12 horse riders who raced around the track. The last rider would have no chair so he was out. That left 11 riders and 10 chairs. The last rider that got a chair was the winner. That year there were 11 cowboys and one cowgirl—her name was Lillian Saverie. She always wore jeans and dressed in cowboy clothes all of the time, even when she clerked at the J.C. Penney store. Well, they got down to two riders and one chair and one of the riders was Lillian. They raced around the track and came to the chair at the same time. There was a big wrestle for the chair and after the dust settled, Lillian had the chair and won the prize. But, the biggest attraction for me was an airplane at the airport. I had saved a long time to afford a ride in a plane and it was my first. So much for the 4th of July of 1933.

July passed very fast and it was almost time to haul lambs. But first we acquired a cab-over International truck that Geryl used on the general freight route. Clarence Grubb, who had a

Ford truck with stock racks like ours, helped haul the lambs. The lamb haul lasted about five weeks that year. The days were very long and I remember Dad and I put in a couple of 24-hour shifts to keep up. After that haul I was exhausted and felt that I could sleep for a week. But, after a night's sleep I was in pretty good shape again.

During the Depression a lot of men were looking at mines that operated in the early 1900s. Some were trying to start up again. I don't remember whether the Clayton Silver Mine was shut down or was just going to install modern machinery. As I remember, Chase Clark[5] was representing Clayton Silver. Their headquarters were in Wallace, Idaho, which was in the rich mining belt in north Idaho. Wallace had several machine shops that made mining machinery, but we didn't haul any machinery from there at that time; although we did haul some machinery, as well as their chemical supplies, from Salt Lake City.

The Clarks

There were three Clark brothers: Chase and Solon were lawyers and Bill was a farmer. I've heard it said that Chase was one of the best lawyers west of the Mississippi. I didn't know much about Solon. I did know Bill and always thought he was the smartest one of the bunch. Mott Clark (who helped Otto Tschanz harvest ice) was, I think, the son of Bill although he was much larger than the other Clarks. Chase had a daughter named Bethine (pronounced Beth-een), who was the same age as Helene (my wife). They spent two summers working together at the Robinson Bar, a resort on the Salmon River. Chase

---

[5] Chase Clark was an attorney, legislator, and federal judge; he served as Idaho's 18th Governor from 1941 to 1943.

Clark owned it. And, by the way, Helene and I later named a daughter Bethene, after Bethine Clark.

Chase Clark had wide circles of influence within the state of Idaho. He later moved to Idaho Falls and became mayor of the city for two terms and later was elected governor of Idaho. He was appointed a federal judge and was located in Spokane, Washington. Chase and Dad always remained good friends. One Sunday afternoon, Helene, our daughter Bethene, and I met Bethine Clark, then Mrs. Frank Church, at Pete and Sandra McDermott's home in Pocatello, Idaho. Sandra is my brother Geryl's daughter. Frank Church was campaigning for reelection to a seat in the United States Senate, but he died of cancer before Election Day. He was ailing when we saw him in Pocatello that Sunday.

My brothers, Dutch and Hilmer, were partners in the Lindburg Truck Line after I moved to Washington and after Dad passed away. I shall relate this as it was told to me by my brothers. They had built the truck line up and were operating several truck trailer and 18-wheeler rigs. That was still in the days when the Interstate Commerce Commission was regulating the transportation industry. The Lindburg Truck Line had permits to haul ore and ore concentrates east to Helena and through Montana and to north Idaho smelters. But they had no permits for back hauls which, I guess, they were doing. Several of their competing carriers with permits in Montana discovered their violations and filed suit against the truck line. The trial was held in Montana in federal court and Chase Clark was the judge. The plaintiffs made their case before the judge, and then it was Hilmer and his lawyer's turn to defend against the charges. Hilmer took the stand and the first thing the judge said to him was "How is your dad? I haven't seen him for a long time." Hilmer then told him that Dad had passed away in 1963 and the judge replied that he was sorry to hear that and he was sorry that he hadn't known about Dad's passing. I guess he also told Hilmer a little about the early days when he lived in Mackay. After that conversation ended, the plaintiff's lawyers asked for a conference with the judge and Hilmer's lawyer. After the conference all charges but one were dropped and to that one Hilmer pleaded guilty and was fined $200. Everything was over except a visit with Judge Clark.

Hauling Fruit

Now to go back to late summer and early fall of 1933. When Dad took a load of cattle to Ogden, I went with him to learn the procedure so I could drive that route. After washing the truck out at the facilities at the stockyards, we loaded several bushels of peaches. Crops on the east side of the Great Salt Lake were mostly fruit. We loaded some pears, cantaloupe, and watermelon. We got the peaches at Mom's request, as she needed some for canning. The fruit in Utah was much cheaper than in Lost River so we had almost a truckload. When we got home, we unloaded the fruit on a large front porch on our house and when word got out about the fruit, it was all sold in less than two days. We sure started something. For a while, the back-haul was fruit. Mom sold it as fast as we brought it in. Because of the short seasons, little fruit could be grown in the Lost River Valley.

Changes at the Truck Line

Our trucking business was growing so fast that some changes had to be made—so we ordered another Dodge truck. It was a 1934 two-ton, extra-long wheelbase that would accommodate a sixteen-foot bed that would haul about a third more than our other trucks. Printed freight bills were ordered—just slips of paper wouldn't do any more—also a typewriter and a second-hand desk. I took on the job of making out the freight bills with Geryl's help, when he wasn't in school. Dad wrote his own by hand. He couldn't wait for us to do it. The Shell Oil dealer owned a small service station in Mackay that wasn't being used and it had a gas pump. We made a deal with him to sell gas to the public for the use of the building as an office. We hired Alvin Gamett to man it and do some bookwork for the truck line.

Mackay didn't have a uniformed policeman in the daytime, but did have a cop that watched the town at night. His name was Courtwright—I don't remember his first name—we knew him as PeeWee. He was very short; I would guess about five-feet five-inches tall, and fairly heavy and very stout. He came to Mackay with the CCC and elected to stay after he got out. He married a local girl and became a citizen of Mackay. He was also Deputy Sheriff for southern Custer County and he was on call in the daytime. He usually wasn't very busy—Mackay being a small town—except for Saturday nights or special functions. He approached us wanting to know if we could use a little help at night. We needed someone part time to take the freight destined for Mackay off the trucks and do the delivery to our customers the next morning. So, we hired him for that and he did a good job for us; he even brought in new business.

Highgrading Stanley Basin

In the Stanley Basin were several men who used to work in the local mines, before they were shut down because there wasn't enough ore to operate at a profit. These men would highgrade some of the mines. To highgrade meant going into a mine that didn't belong to them and, with a pick and any other tools they could use, pick the rich ore out of the veins and sack it to sell to the smelters in Utah. Several of the mines in the area were being highgraded. They would sack the ore and bring it out to where we could pick it up with a truck and take it to the smelter in Utah. It wasn't the best deal for us because we would have a load with several shippers. Although we demanded the bags be securely tagged, we were still responsible to see that each shipper's ore went to the right place.

In one incident that I remember, two of the Franklin brothers and Castro were highgrading the Montana Mine up Jordan Creek as partners. The vein they were working widened out and was yielding a lot of rich ore. One day, Castro went up there alone and was sacking some of the ore. The Franklin brothers didn't trust Castro, so when they didn't find him at his home, they went to the mine and found Castro sacking ore. They accused him of cheating them. They took his shoes, tied him to a beam by his thumbs, and left him. Castro freed himself and walked barefoot about 15 miles over Jordan Creek Summit, through rocks and gravel down to Loon Creek Resort, and called the county sheriff. The Franklin brothers were arrested, convicted, and spent two years in jail. The owners of the mine became more attentive to what was going on in their mine and secured the entrances. The following year, the owners went in and mined the pocket of ore the highgraders had found and got about nine tons of very rich ruby silver. It was so rich that when struck with a hammer it wouldn't shatter but just kind of mashed. They thought so much of their ore that, when I hauled it to the smelter in Garfield, Utah, one of the owners went with me. I guess they wanted to be sure it got there. Ruby silver got its name because, when scratched, the dull silver color turns red like blood.

Hauling Potatoes

I'm not sure of the year, but I think it was the fall of 1933 that the potato market was very poor. We learned that a potato grower was selling 100-pound sacks for 50 cents a sack, excluding the sack, which cost a nickel. We let it be known that after I ran the milk route, we could deliver potatoes in Mackay for a dollar a sack. We sure got a lot of orders so I spent my afternoons loading potatoes at the grower's potato cellar at Moore and hauling them about 20 miles to Mackay. Some of the large families would buy a ton. Most buyers would help me empty the sacks in their winter storage, so I could use the same sacks over and over. They didn't want to pay a nickel for the sack. There were quite a few families still living in the little town of White Knob who wanted potatoes, too, and offered to pay an extra quarter to have me deliver potatoes up there. White Knob was a small settlement of miners that leased the mine even after the company mine shut down. White Knob had a store, a post office, and a school up to grade six. It was located about eight miles west of Mackay on White Knob Mountain. The families who still lived there took about four tons of potatoes. During the Depression, potatoes and beans were the main diet for the majority of the population.

The rest of 1933 was quite uneventful, but as Christmas drew near it became bitter cold. Trucking then was quite a challenge. The trucks were hard to start, and the milk would freeze in the cans, which made the cheesemaker hard to get along with, as he would have to use steam to thaw the ice from inside of the cans. If I remember right, it was that year when antifreeze became available. It wasn't too satisfactory, but better than nothing at all. We had to watch it, as it would boil out once in a while.

It seemed that time passed by fast and Christmas was here. We had the usual Christmas. I might mention that before we had electricity we used candles with candleholders that attached to the branches of the tree. The candle wax would run down the candle onto the tree. Thinking back, it's a wonder we didn't have a tree fire—although I never heard of a tree fire in those days.

New Year's Day was bright, clear, and cold. There were no holidays on the milk route; it had to be hauled every day, even on Christmas. I think that was the reason we had our Christmas in the evening—always too much to do in the morning.

The next job was ice harvest; no different from last year except the Hayspur Fish Hatchery had Otto Sr. cut ice for them. If I remember right, they ordered about 50 tons. I'd haul ice for Otto but the last load of the day was hauled for Hayspur. It was about a 60-mile haul so it would be dark when I got there. Hayspur Hatchery is on the Wood River. From Mackay it was down through Arco, across the Craters of the Moon, and through Carey on Highway 20, past Picabo about a mile. Then north two miles. When I arrived there was always a crew to unload me so I didn't have anything to do but watch. I spent very little time there. I'd get back to Carey where I would eat supper. Then in two and a half hours I'd be home. The road across the Craters wasn't as straight as it is now. It would wind up every little canyon to get around the lava flow and it was dirt and very rough. I don't remember how many trips I made, but it seemed I made a trip every day that they cut ice. Then ice harvest was over and the most unusual thing about it was I don't believe Otto fell into the pond. If he did, I didn't hear about it.

Bridge Construction

The road was being built on the Salmon River. They started at the foot of Galena Summit on the Salmon side, at the very head of the river. It was as modern as it is today, only it wasn't paved. It was built down below Sunbeam when I first went to Stanley. Contracts were let for more than a section at a time, so there were always a couple of contractors working. Morrison Knudson had the contract to build the bridge across the river at Slate Creek and we had the job of hauling the reinforcing steel. In those days, there was no ready-mix cement;

everything had to be done at the bridge site. The gravel and sand was mined, washed, and piled. It was washed by high-pressure pumps on huge screens fed by conveyor belts to elevate the material to the top of the screens. The holes were dug by hand and pilings were driven to keep the river bottom from caving in and the water out, although what water ran in was pumped out with pumps powered by gasoline engines. When the holes were dug, forms were put in place. The reinforcing steel was installed and then the cement poured for the pilings and abutments of the bridge. The cement was mixed right at the bridge site by a big mixer with a large scoop attached that held the same amount as the mixer's capacity. The mix had to be just right—so much sand, so much gravel, so much cement, and so much water. The mix was carried to the forms out in the middle of the river by a traveling belt (probably a poor expla-nation but it seems the best I can do). The cement came in pa-per bags that weighed 94 pounds to the bag.

A fellow I didn't know got the bid to haul the cement. He bid on hauling it in from Inkom, a cement manufacturing plant. He had an old truck that would haul about 1,300 bags or 6-½ tons. He was the only driver and he had nothing but trouble trying to keep the engine cool—it was always running hot and steaming. Normally fans are on the backside of the radiator but that didn't keep the engine cool. So, he took it to a shop and had a fan installed in front of the radiator. Now he had two fans—one in front and one behind. Sure made a funny looking rig and the engine still heated up. He asked us to haul a load for him once in a while so he could keep up. His troubles were first, his truck, and second, he didn't know how to drive in the mountains. In the heat of the day the air is light and moves up the mountain, so if you are pulling up hill you will have a tail wind that prevents the radiator from getting enough air to keep the engine cool. In the cool of the night the air is heavier and comes down the mountain, so the radiator gets a good supply of cool air that keeps the engine cool. It is best to drive the mountain roads at night, especially with heavy loads. You could get by with light loads or an empty one anytime of the day.

Hauling Cement

Our new truck was delivered and Dad was busy building a 16-foot bed on it. He finished it just in time to haul wool. It would have the biggest load that we had to date. 1934 was going pretty fast—hauling first lambs, then cattle (some went to Ogden with salt coming back for the cattle associations). The lumber yards in Mackay and Arco were ordering quite a bit of cement that we hauled from Inkom, which was on the road below Pocatello about ten miles.

A hard lesson was learned on my first trip to the cement plant to get a load. The paper sacks that held the cement were received by the cement plant empty and with both ends closed. They were filled by a hollow metal finger that was one inch in diameter and eight inches long. It was inserted in the sack between the closed ends and the sack body. The sack filled by cement being blown through the hollow finger. Each sack was then dropped into the chute, with a sharp drop to the truck that was backed under the lower end of the chute. I was standing at the end of the chute waiting for the first sack with my arms outstretched. Here came a sack of cement at a good rate of speed that struck me in the midsection, backed me up, and set me on my bottom while other sacks of cement piled up all around me. I was in a panic. When the sacks stopped coming, the man that was filling the sacks came down to help me straighten out the mess and showed me how to load cement. I found out you don't stand in front of the chute, but stand on the side of the chute and guide the sack to where you want it to go. When the front end of the truck is full, you holler to the man who is filling the sacks. He stops the sacks so you can move the truck ahead a bit and resume loading until fully loaded.

Moving a Dredge

In November of 1934, a couple of men approached Dad. They said they had a contract to move a dredge to the Yankee Fork of the Salmon River and wanted us to help them move it. They had two Ford trucks that they would load. All we had to do was drive to the dredge site. I doubt they had looked the roads over before they bid the job. It was paved for only five miles to the foot of the Mackay Dam Hill. The road from there over Willow Creek Summit was the same route as it is today, only it was gravel and very rough. After getting down from Willow Creek Summit, you leave Highway 93 and go across a sagebrush flat for about five miles and then start to climb up into Spar Canyon. It's kind of a steep pull for about four or five miles to the top of the hill, and then a gentle slope down toward the East Fork of the Salmon River. It was a dirt, single-track road with turnouts. There is a deep canyon with sharp turns toward the lower end just before the East Fork. Then the road goes down the East Fork to the Salmon River and then up the left side of the river. It's also a narrow single track with turnouts. In places the mountains come right down to the river. There the road is built in cuts called "dugways" with vertical walls. The old road stayed on the left side of the river until it crossed the river on an old steel bridge at Grave Yard Hill, about two miles below Clayton. A steep climb brought you up to a narrow dugway all the way through Clayton onto a narrow, single-track road for about a mile, then across another steel bridge to the left side of the river, then on a single-track road until you get to Slate Creek Bridge. That's as far as the new road had been built down the river. After crossing the bridge, the road is wide and well graded but kind of rough all the way to Yankee Fork. Then it goes up a little hill to the Sunbeam Store, where a single-track, unimproved road went about five miles to the dredge site. The road up the Yankee Fork had a very narrow Forest Service bridge on a sharp turn. In fact, the road up the Yankee Fork was a Forest Service road. The distance from Mackay to the dredge site was about 85 miles.

When the dredge parts began arriving at the rail head in Mackay, we learned there would be six trucks hauling: two of ours, two belonging to the men who had the contract, one Ford from the Standard Oil dealer driven by Carl Wall, and another owned and driven by Clarence Grubb. To unload the machinery from the rail cars to the trucks, they set up a gin pole. A gin pole is a sturdy pole about 20 feet long with the lower end in a shallow hole in the ground, braced on both sides. It was positioned about 10 feet from the rail car. It had a cable on the backside attached to a heavy hand-winch anchored securely to the ground. It also had a loose cable extending over the rail car to keep the pole from tipping over. A series of cables and pulleys with one pulley anchored to the ground could attach to a truck that furnished the power to do the lifting. It worked fairly well and was the only way to get the machinery out of a gondola rail car if you didn't have a crane.

We were planning to make a trip a day. We would leave Mackay early in the morning and try to get back to Mackay in the early afternoon so we'd be ready to go the next morning. It didn't always work that way. We were getting a little snow on the Salmon River. It wasn't much of a bother except on the single-track roads, where the wheels ran continuously in the tracks and the warm tires turned the snow to ice. It was no problem as long as the front wheels stayed down in the bottom of the cupped track. But, if they climbed up the side and then suddenly slipped back it would give you a thrill. That's what happened one morning when I was following the Grubb truck between East Fork and Graveyard Hill. I think Grubb was nervous on that narrow road so he kept trying to get as far away from the river as possible. His front wheels would climb up the icy side of the track and then would slip down in the bottom. I guess he lost his nerve and stopped his truck. I stopped and went up to see what his trouble was. It was a tight squeeze to get between his truck and the mountainside. When I got up to the cab, Grubb stated that he wasn't going to drive the truck another inch. I finally convinced him to let me drive to a wide spot in the road so the rest of us could get by. He finally agreed, got in with me, and rode up to the dredge site, where we unloaded. Then he rode with me back to Mackay. The next morning George Wall rode with me and drove Grubb's truck to the dredge site, unloaded it, and took it back to Mackay. I don't remember Grubb hauling any more of that dredge.

The pontoons started coming on flat cars and we just slid them off of the rail cars onto the trucks with rollers and bars. There was one pontoon that had part of the super structure welded onto it. It was the biggest piece of the dredge. Although it was big, its weight wasn't a problem. As I remember, it only weighed about four tons. Bulk was the problem. It was sixteen feet long, seven feet wide, and six feet deep. The attached super structure was about twelve feet long. It couldn't be loaded upright because it would be so high that it would catch phone lines and other lines that crossed the roads. So, it laid on its side so the welded piece stuck out the right side. It was loaded onto the 1934 Dodge truck that I was driving. I really had no trouble until I came to the first steel bridge. I was glad Dad was behind me. He left his truck and guided me across the bridge that was just six inches wider that the load. After crossing the bridge, I pulled up the hill onto the dugway—about two miles from Clayton. There the trouble started. Now the high vertical bank was to my right and the road wasn't quite wide enough to accommodate the load. The piece that was welded to the pontoon was digging into the bank. Dad got in front of me and told me to turn a little to my left. Looking out the door window, I could see nothing but the river 300 feet below me. But I trusted him and we got past that tight place. At the next tight place we weren't so lucky. We had to pick the bank out to get by. As we started to do that, a crew from the dredge arrived to help. It took nearly three hours to go the two miles into Clayton. We had no more trouble until the right angle turn onto the next steel bridge. This was negotiated in about half an hour. Then we were on the left side of the river with the steel arm extending out and sometimes over the river. About a half mile below Sullivan Hot Springs, the road was built under a solid rock cliff. Our load was too high to get under it and the road under us was also solid rock. The rock ledge sloped right to the water's edge. We were really stuck. The road only had to be widened about 4 feet for about 200 feet. The problem was solved when the dredge crew arrived with two trucks of rock and a Cat with a bulldozer. We left the old road at Slate Creek and traveled on the new road to Sunbeam. We arrived at the Sunbeam store about eleven o'clock that night but decided to go on up to the dredge site and stay in the bunkhouse until morning. Going up Yankee Fork was very slow until we got to the Forest Service bridge. It was too narrow to cross. That was the last straw. I was sure tired. Dad and I had been on the road 18 hours in the cold with only a couple of sandwiches to eat. I was ready to call it quits and sleep in the cab until morning. But that wasn't to be. There was nothing to do but dismantle the right side of the bridge. Some of the dredge employees were still behind us, so we all pitched in and it took an hour to remove the right-side railings. We crossed the bridge and crawled on to the dredge site and finally into bed in the bunkhouse.

After three hours sleep we were called for breakfast. It was hard to leave that bed. To our surprise we knew the cook. He was kind of a jack-of-all-trades but cooking wasn't one of them. We concluded that after partaking of his cuisine.

It didn't take long to get unloaded and back to Mackay for another load. We got to Mackay about eleven o'clock and loaded that afternoon ready to go early the next morning. The weather had moderated the next day and it had turned quite cloudy as the five trucks left for the dredge. The trip was uneventful until we got to Slate Creek and on the new road. Then it started to snow. And, snow it did. I don't think I had ever seen it come down like that. We went about three miles—I was in the lead—and as I was rounding a curve and going up a sharp incline I slide off the curve toward the river. In that three miles it snowed 15 to 18 inches. We were stuck. It stopped snowing as abruptly as it had started and it began to clear and get cold. Clyde Torrey, who had a few cabins and a little store about a quarter mile up the road, waded through the snow to tell us a snowplow was on its way from Stanley. It would be some time before it arrived so we all followed him back to his store and waited for the plow. It arrived just as it was getting dark. The operators had seen several cars stalled along the road. They said that they would go down to Slate Creek and turn around and would help us on their way back. So we walked back to the trucks. As soon as we started our trucks, they arrived to pull us back onto the road and then followed us to Sunbeam. We found that the Caterpillar had cleared the road up Yankee Fork. He stayed at Sunbeam and waited for us. It was a good thing he did because the hill from the highway up to the store was so slick we had to have help getting up there. We arrived at the dredge site without further problems, although there was a foot more snow at the dredge than there was down on the river. We unloaded and got back to Mackay at 1:30 the next morning. The snow ended at Clayton and it was clear the rest of the way home.

The last load, the engine and generator, were a little bit too heavy for the smaller trucks so I got the honor. I had a helper that trip. His name was Albert Saviera. It was a bright, sunny day and we made the trip without incident. We were unloaded by 3:30 p.m. The sun had just left the valleys but was still shining brightly on the south and west sides of the mountains. Satisfied that we had finished a long and tedious job, we started for home. We had gone scarcely a mile before we found a huge snow slide blocking the road. We backed up, turned around, drove back to the dredge, and reported the slide. The Cat and dozer went to clear the slide. The road at that particular place was only a few feet above the creek and the slide had partially dammed it up. So, there was no place to push the snow except move it up and down the road—then into the creek. It was a slow process. At eleven o'clock he was still working, so we decided to stay the night in the bunkhouse. That was a wise decision because the road wasn't cleared until three in the morning.

We were up for breakfast. Baxter Lightfoot was still the cook and things hadn't improved much since we last ate there. My helper, Albert, exclaimed as we were leaving the mess hall that Baxter Lightfoot was the only person he knew who could case-harden an egg. We were back to Mackay shortly after noon. The job was complete.

This is not the dredge that stands in the Yankee Fork today, but is an earlier one built by the Yuba Company in California. It only had 3-cubic-foot buckets and weighed about 350 tons, whereas the one in Yankee Fork today has 8-cubic-foot buckets and weighs 1,000 tons. Although the pond was dug, this dredge was never set up. The reasons were that it was too small and couldn't dig deep enough and it could never handle the big aggregate in the Yankee Fork. It was hauled back out and stored in Hailey, Idaho. From there it was moved to Elk City where it worked very successfully. It was bought by the people that have a large museum in Nevada City, Montana. Maybe you can visit it there someday.

The company that was responsible for that dredge took the name of the Snake River Mining Company. They bought up all of the mining claims in the Yankee Fork from Pole Creek Campground to the mouth of Jordan Creek, an area about seven miles long and as wide as the canyon. The man in charge of the project was Mr. Salt. He had a very British dialect and all. I remember Dad saying that he and Mr. Salt were figuring some weights that didn't come out right, so Dad said it looks like you made a mistake. Mr. Salt replied, "I never make a mistake—maybe an error but never a mistake." I wasn't very familiar with the company but I understood that the money for the company came from California. When Mr. Salt was down there on a business trip, he was killed in a car-train wreck. That was about all I ever heard about that dredge.

The deep snow and cold weather had just about stopped all activities on the Salmon River from Slate Creek on up to and including Yankee Fork and Stanley Basin, and all the way to Galena Summit and beyond. I don't think there were a hundred people all together staying there in the winter. We hauled a little ice for the Sunbeam Store (about 50 tons, I would guess), most of the time from Little Redfish Lake. All the sawing and loading was done by hand, so we only made one trip a day. I never got in on that haul. Dad did it, and Geryl helped on his Christmas vacation from school. That was the last year they hauled from Little Redfish Lake. The following year their ice was obtained from the pond that the dredge people left on the Yankee Fork. Keeping the road open between the store and the dredge pond wasn't too much of a problem, but beyond that, snowshoes or skis were the chief modes of transportation.

The problems with the new road that they were building down the Salmon River was that rocks on the hillsides kept rolling down on the road. It was especially bad when the weather warmed up or the wind was blowing. The state highway department would make a couple trips a day to plow the rocks off. They still caused accidents as they often came down while vehicles were driving by. The worst place was where the road was dug out of a solid rock cliff. Just across the river from Robinson Bar there were about four gullies on the face of the mountain. In the winter or early spring, small snow slides would come down the gullies, spilling onto the road and blocking it. They came down mostly in the evenings. If that happened while you were trying to drive through there, you would have to get your pick and shovel and dig your way through it. It was hard digging because snow slides bring down rock, trees and anything else in its path. Geryl got caught in one that smashed the left front fender of the truck. It took him three hours to dig himself out. He straightened the fender just enough so it wouldn't rub on the tire when he turned the wheel, then he came on home. The next day I worked on the fender—straightened it out to be passable but it looked awful rough, so we ordered a new one. A few days later it came in but we were busy so we just laid it aside. We never got around to putting it on until the next winter. The very next trip up the Salmon River, at the same place, another slide pretty much demolished the new fender. Sometimes you just can't win.

Sunbeam Dam

A very promising mine was on Jordan Creek, which drains into Yankee Fork about ten miles from Sunbeam. The mine itself is about eighteen miles from Sunbeam. In 1909, when Sunbeam Dam was built, there was no road up Yankee Fork. The only way to reach the Sunbeam Mine, Custer, and Bonanza was the stage road from Challis or from the Stanley Basin up Stanley Creek to Kelley Creek, then over the summit down Sawmill Canyon to Yankee Fork, below Bonanza. That was a trail used to pack hay grown in the Stanley Basin into the Custer area for the horses. It also was used to drive cattle into the Custer area. Because there was no refrigeration in those days, cattle were driven in, then slaughtered for meat as needed. It was said that 5,000 to 6,000 people were living in Custer, Bonanza, and the Sunbeam Mine area, so energy was premium. The only alternative to electricity was steam and it took a lot of logs to generate steam, so the mountains were quite bare around the mine. It was decided that a dam would be built on the Salmon River and a power line built from the dam to the mine; a distance of about 20 miles. All of the materials had to be freighted using teams and freight wagons from Corrine, Utah, to the Sunbeam Dam site. From there, packhorses delivered materials for the power line. In fact, all of the equipment and materials were packed in for the Sunbeam Mine as well as the Custer mines before the wagon road was built. Horace Lewis, grandfather of Ken Lewis, who has a grape vineyard and orchard north of Prosser, Washington, built the wagon road. Horace Lewis freighted with a 20-horse team hitched to 3 wagons. They are now in a museum at Ketchum, Idaho. The Sunbeam Dam was completed in 1909 and in 1910 the Sunbeam Mine went broke. The dam produced no power after that. The dam remained intact for more than 29 years.

In the early 1930s, the Idaho Fish and Game Department breached the dam so the salmon could migrate upstream as they did before the dam was built. The modern biologists suggest that the lakes in the Stanley Basin were the primary spawning areas for the sockeye salmon on the Salmon River. However, during the twenty-some years that the dam was intact, my belief is that very few, if any, salmon ever made it over the dam. It was and is my belief, which is shared by other residents of the

Salmon River Valley, both of my generation and the generation before, that very few sockeye salmon ever made it up the river, especially above Challis.[6] I only heard of two being caught. They were very sparse and choice eating and it was news up and down the river. Since the dam was breached, a lot of Chinook salmon migrate up river. Today, they arrive at a modern fish hatchery built in the 1990s, about two miles above Redfish Creek.

1935

1935 arrived bright, clear, and cold with very little snow on the ground. The heavy snow that fell on the Salmon River never extended to the Lost Rivers. We still had drought. When I got off the milk route we all sat down to a big turkey dinner. After dinner we reviewed last year's operations and were quite pleased with the results. Buying trucks took a good share of our income and as a result the cash flow was pretty tight. Dad's reasoning was if you're going to get the jobs, you have to have the equipment.

Frozen Cargo

The next two weeks were pretty slow, as I remember. Of course, the milk route ran steady. The one problem we had with the general freight in cold weather was keeping the beer, some of the canned goods, and the fresh produce from freezing. Although we could deliver in Arco, Moore, and Darlington—and if not too late, Leslie—the rest of the load was stored in a heated garage in Mackay. The driver had to get back to Darlington to

---

[6] Mac Tschanz, Roland's brother-in-law, says that Rol didn't understand that the sockeye salmon from which Redfish lakes take their name don't migrate up the Salmon River above Challis.

sleep and then drive back the next morning to Mackay to continue the route to Challis and Stanley. The Bohemian Beer distributor chose us to deliver beer to all of their customers from Midway and all points along our route to Challis and Stanley. Sometimes we would have a whole load of beer and it froze very easily. Before we learned how to prevent that problem we lost some of the load. You knew you were in trouble when you heard the bottles popping. The beer froze easily because in the first days after prohibition was lifted, 3.2 percent beer was the only alcoholic beverage legally sold. It seemed that beer joints were springing up everywhere and a lot of beer was consumed. I guess a person had to drink so much to get that good feeling.

Homemade School Bus

There were so many kids from Leslie and Darlington and from other families living below Mackay that they had a meeting to see about getting a bus to haul the kids to high school in Mackay. I guess they contacted the school district but didn't get any money because of the financial difficulty of just keeping the school running. The district couldn't stand any expense such as starting bus routes. They felt they would need three or four buses to service all the outlying areas. So, the families between Darlington and Mackay decided to go on their own. They asked Dad if he would be interested in running it. Because Hilmer started high school in the fall of 1934, he was elected to drive. He would drive the bus to school in the mornings, attend school, and then drive it back after school in the evenings. As I remember, someone rustled up an old bus body. It had windows and benches. It was a square box that looked like it was made for a wagon or sleigh. Dad found a 1932 Ford truck at a dealer in Blackfoot with a damaged cab. The dealer agreed to take the cab off, leaving the windshield, and mount the old body described above. Now they had a school bus. I don't remember the financial arrangement, but it seemed satisfactory and also provided Hilmer and Dutch a way to school.

Hauling Construction Material

The first of February, the state highway department let contracts for two more sections of the Salmon River road. That would bring the new road down to Clayton. The Continental Oil Company got the contract to furnish the petroleum products for both contractors. Although the contracts were let in February, the actual work didn't get underway until March as they had to move in their equipment. Because there were no facilities on the Salmon River they had to set up a dining hall, including a kitchen, for all of their employees. We hauled most of the construction material for both contractors. The lumber came from the local sawmills. We hauled the hardware in from a hardware warehouse in Pocatello. It became obvious we would need another truck and driver, so we went to Blackfoot to order a heavy duty Dodge truck like the one we bought the year before—only it had a shorter wheel base. We looked at the list of driver applicants and chose Dewey Dickson. When our truck arrived it was red; not exactly what we ordered. But, we took it anyway. When buying trucks, we would buy chassis and cab only and build our own beds. That was what Dad and Dewey did for the next three or four days.

The next improvement was leasing space in a brick warehouse from Frank Stacy, the owner and operator of Stacy's Department Store, the biggest store in town. It sold everything from a full line of groceries to hardware, dry goods, and clothing. He was one of our best customers. Stacy also was the dealer for DuPont Dynamite and had a powder house with triple steel doors and walls that were five bricks thick. Each door had a different key. All the explosives were shipped by rail. We would unload the boxcars and haul the explosives to the powder house.

Hauling Tungsten

One Sunday, as I was working on one of the trucks and Hilmer was trying to close some of the spaces where cold air was getting into the old school bus, a man pulled into the yard. He was well dressed and drove an expensive car. Generally, when someone drove into the yard they were after a bag of salt, as we always kept some on hand. But this fellow didn't seem to be that type. The man came over to where I was working and introduced himself as W.P. Barton. He asked if my brother was around so I sent him over to where Hilmer was working. Well, Hilmer wasn't the brother he wanted to see. After talking to him for a while, we realized it was Dad he wanted to see. Dad wasn't home so we offered to take a message for him and told him that we expected Dad home in an hour or so. He said he'd be back in a couple of hours. Mr. Barton returned about ten minutes after Dad got home and we found out what he wanted. He had a tungsten mine near Patterson in the Pahsimeroi Valley, about two miles up Patterson Creek. He had an ore mill and had concentrated 20 tons that he wanted to ship to New Jersey, the only market for tungsten in the United States. At that time, tungsten was controlled by the Chinese; they had the patent on tungsten smelting.

The Pahsimeroi Valley runs parallel with Big Lost River Valley. The Pahsimeroi River flows north into Salmon River about 20 miles below Challis, whereas the Big Lost River flows south into the Arco Desert. The Lost River Mountain Range separates the Pahsimeroi east of the mountains and Lost River on the west. The Pahsimeroi Valley is quite wide on the upper end and narrows the last few miles near the mouth. There are three settlements in the valley with post offices. Ellis is located where the river joins the Salmon. Fifteen miles upriver is May, the largest, which has the only school (eight grades). Then about ten miles on up river is Patterson, located on Patterson Creek. It was estimated to be a 50-mile haul and half of it was just a trail through the sagebrush and over Doublesprings, an 8,500-foot-plus pass between Lost River and Pahsimeroi Valley, just north of Mount Borah. This would be the short route. The long route would be over Willow Creek Summit through Challis down river to Ellis, then up the Pahsimeroi River to Patterson. That route was more than 100 miles. We chose the shorter route.

It took four truckloads to move the 20 tons. The concentrates were in small burlap bags about 15 inches tall and 12 inches in diameter and tied with wire ties with enough bag above the ties to get a hold of them. Each weighed 100 pounds and the bags were extremely dirty—coal black dirt. So, we tried not to get our clothes dirty by grasping the top of the bag. I tried to lift the first one using only one hand, then two hands—then I decided it was frozen to the floor before I finally used enough effort and lifted it. To transfer them to the rail car, we had to lift them up, set them in the doorway, and then use a lift truck to wheel them to the end of the car. It was two days before the job was done. I guess he liked our work, as he became one of our better customers.

We gained a new customer while working in the Pahsimeroi Valley: the Woods Livestock Company. They were about ten miles downriver from the road to Patterson, on the west side of the river. They owned a couple thousand acres of bottom land along the river. They grew pasture and wild hay. We hauled bulk corn to them that was shipped into Mackay by rail from Nebraska.

Then there were the cracked beans we hauled from the elevators around the Twin Falls area to the sheep men. They were in bulk so we built sideboards to handle them.

First Semi

We had several hauling jobs and we were busy trying to keep up. On a trip to Salt Lake City, Dad stopped at the Long Manufacturing and Fabricating Company and ordered a semi-trailer built to Dad's specifications. It would be eighteen feet long. The first six feet would be high enough to clear the truck it would be mounted on, and the last twelve feet was one foot lower for stability. But, it required wheel wells to clear the rear wheels. They turned out to be a pain in the neck, but we made them work. It was rounded in front with a steel nose for wind resistance, which was one of its good features. When it was finished I went to get it. The bed of the truck had to be taken off so the fifth wheel could be mounted on it. The truck was just the cab and chassis. I got there just as they were opening. They went to work equipping the truck with the brake controls and mounting the fifth wheel. About three o'clock in the afternoon they were ready to mount the trailer on the truck. After checking everything out it was time to back it out of the building. The building was long with a center isle and only one end had a door. Of course, they built the trailer with its front end facing the solid wall. It was a tight squeeze getting the truck to the front of the trailer to hook it up. I had no experience backing a semi-trailer, but I was willing to try. After several tries I could see that I just couldn't back it straight. After pulling forward and trying several more times, one of Long's employees decided to try and had no better luck that I did. Another employee also tried and was no better than we were. It was quitting time so they decided to leave my truck and trailer there overnight. I didn't get much sleep that night worrying about getting that rig

Geryl, Hilmer, Edythe, Cecil (Dad), Dutch, and Roland

out of that building. I was up early, had my breakfast, and was down there before they opened. When they arrived to open up, I got in the truck and after a few tries I had if half way out but it was too close to one side of the door. After a couple more tries I finally had the whole thing out. I suppose the owner of the business thought he was lucky to have a building left and I felt as if I just escaped from a vicious animal. I also worried about how I was going to get out of the city trouble free. There was a truck stop where we fueled that had a big piece of land behind the station. I drove there and practiced handling the rig until I thought I could get by. I gassed up and started for home. I got through Ogden okay and then had to stop down by the lake to load salt that we bought from a farmer who scraped the salt up and sacked it. He helped me load eight tons. I got home late that night, very tired, but wiser.

Geryl and Otto Tschanz Jr. graduated from school that spring and Hilmer was out of school for the summer, so that was a big help. The general freight business was picking up because of the two contractors and all of the activity on the Salmon River. The Clayton Hotel in Clayton was in the way of the new road. It was such an old and dilapidated building that it was considered better to tear it down and build a new building. We had the job of hauling the supplies for the new building, except the rough framing lumber that was procured from local saw mills (they delivered their own product). Because there were no finishing mills in the area, we hauled all of the finished lumber. We also hauled all of the hardware, windows, and so forth. The building was large with a kitchen, a large dining room, and a post office and service station on the ground floor. The second story was all sleeping rooms.

There seemed to be a lot of interest in the old mining dumps that were left by the mines that operated in the late 1800s and early 1900s. The recovery in those days was poor so new assays showed enough value that it paid to ship them to be milled and smelted. And so, we put sheet iron floors in two of the trucks because the ore had to be shoveled by hand from the trucks into gondola rail cars. A man in Mackay unloaded the trucks and the shippers generally loaded for us. Once we started to load a rail car, we had to load it in three days or the rail company would charge demurrage of three dollars a day. We tried to never let that happen.

CCC Contract

We learned that the government was asking for bids to haul commodities from their warehouse in Pocatello to the thirteen CCC camps they served. The camps were on the Salmon River, Big Lost River, Snake River, and Rock Creek, and another up a canyon out of Logan, Utah. Dad asked Otto Tschanz Jr. and me to figure the mileage from Pocatello to each of the camps. Otto was in his last semester of high school so we worked nights.

That left me free to help with wool hauling during the day. It took a week to figure the mileage; then we figured the dollar amount we needed per mile with a five-ton load per trip to each camp once a week. We were to haul all of their needs except petroleum products, explosives, fresh meats, and fresh produce. We were to have the bids in by the first of June and if we won the bid, the job started the first of July. We got the bid in on time.

We were awarded the CCC contract. We were trying to devise a plan to coordinate with the warehouse shipping days to each camp so we could combine two camps in the same area in one load, if possible. Dad left it up to me to see if something could be worked out. I met with the person who was the head of shipping and took care of the orders sent in from the various camps. For example, the camps at Paul and Rock Creek could be one load as the road to Rock Creek went right by Paul. Paul was about five miles north of Burley and Rock Creek about 30 miles south of Burley, almost to the Nevada border. The camps at Pass Creek, Wild Horse Creek and the camp out on the Arco Desert were close enough to be worked in with general freight. The same was true with the Yankee Fork camp. The camp in Utah was a loner and couldn't be combined with any other camp. The rest could be easily managed as they were down Salmon City and North Fork way. The trips were to run weekly with an extra load sometimes. If that happened we were given two days' notice. Things were working out pretty well. Geryl, Dewey, and I were getting well acquainted with the routes. We had one major problem. We weren't getting paid. One month went by and no check. Another month went by, no check. I asked the manager of the warehouse why we weren't getting paid and he said he'd check for me. Two weeks later I checked with him again. Four months passed and no money. In the fifth month we got our first monthly check. For the rest of the year the government was four months behind in its payments.

When the first year contract was coming to a close, the manager of the warehouse asked us to bid again. We told him we were reluctant because we still had four months' pay coming. He told me whenever you bid on a government job always give them a discount for prompt payment. We bid for another year and we raised our amounts and included a 1% discount if payment was received by the tenth of the following month. That was what it took. The next year our payments were received before the tenth, as they should be.

With increasing general freight and the CCC contract, we needed another truck—something enclosed to protect the freight from the weather. The place where we bought most of our equipment had an International truck and semi-trailer van. This was what we were looking for. The van was 16 feet long, nearly 8 feet wide, and was 7½ feet floor to roof. The front end was rounded to cut wind resistance. The rig was repossessed from a man who was trying to get a permit to haul general freight from Pocatello to Blackfoot, Moreland, and the towns in the Lost River Valley. After a year, he went broke. We got the rig for what was owed on it. It was still good even if the truck was under-powered and was so slow that no one wanted to drive it. We put up with it until we could get a truck with more power. The CCC haul was settling down very well with Geryl and Dewey driving. Once in a while, some of the rest of us had to help with an extra load.

Hauling Cattle

My next job was hauling cattle from the range down to the owner ranches. I'm going to take this space to tell about the cattle drives from the Stanley Basin, which was a very large area that supported several thousand head of cattle during the summer and early fall. Still, the grass grew as high as a cow's belly when it came time to take the cattle down river to Challis and the surrounding area ranches known as Round Valley. The cattle ranchers belonged to the Challis Cattlemen Association, which was said to be the biggest association of its kind in the United States. After a few days, the whole 60 miles between Stanley Basin and Challis would be full of cattle. There would be cowboys herding them along and keeping them off the ranches along the river. With so many cattle it was impossible to keep track of them all. They lost some to rustlers. It was nearly impossible to travel on the Salmon River road during the week or ten days of the drive. Once the cattle were on the ranches, the owners separated the cows they wanted to keep from the cattle ready for market. The market cattle would be trucked to the railhead. There the cattle would be sold to the buyers who would weigh them and settle with owners. Some owners had us haul their cattle to Ogden and took a chance on the market. Doc Phelps was one of them but he always wanted his cattle sold in one lot. That meant holding the first load until all were hauled. The easiest way for us to do that would be to run the largest truck 24 hours a day to Ogden. Dad would drive the truck to Challis, load cattle and drive back to Mackay. Then two of us would take over and drive to Ogden and back to Mackay. That way we made the trip to Ogden and back to Challis every 24 hours. It took eight days to move all of Dr. Phelps' cattle, hauling about 12 head to the load. He claimed he got more money for his cattle that way instead of selling to buyers at Mackay. Two years in a row, Otto Jr. helped me on the drive to Ogden. Several cattlemen sent their cattle to Ogden so we kept one truck busy. Dr. Phelps was the only one who wanted to sell all of his cattle at once, so we were not so rushed with the other hauls. It was inconvenient to back-haul loads in the stock racks, but we managed.

My Worst Haul

One of the most harassing hauls I ever had was when we moved a Taylor family from Pahsimeroi into the Middle Fork wilderness area. The only way to get to where they were moving was to fly in or pack in with horses. We were to move their household belongings and machinery down to Big Creek head-quarters. From there, they would pack their belongings the rest of the way. They had several herds of cattle driven in by Morgan Creek down to wherever their place was. He said that one truck was all that was needed to haul all of his stuff, so Geryl and I got to his place about noon to start loading. After a while it be-came apparent that another truck was needed, so we called Dad and he came with the red Dodge that he drove most of the time. When he arrived we had finished loading our truck—including a crate of chickens on top of the cab and the pet cat in a card-board box that we kept in the cab with us. It was quite a job loading the rest of their belongings on Dad's truck. It was about 75 miles to Stanley so we stopped there to eat. It was a good thing we did because that was the last thing we ate for more than 24 hours, except for a couple of candy bars we had with us. It was well after dark when we started through the wilder-ness area for Big Creek headquarters. We didn't know where we were going, but the Forest Service road led there. Being late in the fall, it hadn't been graded and wasn't in the best shape. It made going quite slow. We were lucky to average 30 miles per hour.

We thought we could get to the village of Yellow Pine, catch a little sleep, have breakfast, and go on in daylight. But, that was not to be. About 30 miles out of Stanley in Bear Valley, the truck broke through a bridge that spanned a small creek with about six to eight inches of water in it. The bridge was about ten to twelve feet long and, luckily, just the right back wheel broke through. The only thing to do was to jack up that side of the truck. We built a makeshift platform to place the jack and, to keep our feet dry, we stood on rocks and broken timbers from the bridge. After a couple of hours we got the truck on dry ground but Dad's truck still had to cross the creek. It took another hour, working with hand shovels and moving rock, to make a place where Dad could ford the creek. We were dead tired but on our way again. We got over the Bear Valley–Deadwood summit about three o'clock. We were so tired we decided to stop and sleep for a while. I always carried a bedroll on my truck when I was out on mountain roads. Motels were few and far between. A bedroll consisted of a piece of canvas and a couple of blankets. I hadn't even heard of sleeping bags in those days. Geryl and I used the bed roll and Dad slept in his truck. We stopped in the middle of the road. No one was dumb enough to drive those roads that time of night. While we were asleep it started to rain. We were under the back of my truck but were out far enough that we got rained on a little. I decided that I could fix that. I left a rope loose from the truck tarp when I took the bedroll out. I figured that if I just pulled on that, it would extend out far enough to keep us dry. I gave the rope a jerk and the water that had accumulated on the tarp poured down on us. Geryl thought that was a dumb thing I'd done and I guess it was. Now we were wet and soon would be cold.

It was a little after daybreak when we got underway again. We stopped at the Landmark Ranger Station to report the broken bridge. We had gone just a few miles farther when disaster struck again. A chuckhole in the road caused the fan to hit the radiator and the water leaked out. We had to stop and try to fix it. That is a repair that needs a shop, but here we were somewhere near the middle of nowhere. I had some hardening gasket material so we plastered that into the core of the radiator around the leak, hoping that was a cure. But, first it had to dry (that generally took about 12 hours). We couldn't wait that long. Geryl suggested we put heat on it. Tempers were a little short and I asked him to blow on it. He had a better idea: wrap a stick with a rag, pour a little gas on it, and set it on fire. That sounded like it would work, but the only way to get the heat to the gasket material was to start the engine and let the fan draw the heat around it. The radiator had no water in it but we could run the engine a minute or two without damaging it. That's what we did and, what you do know, it worked. We straightened the fan so it wouldn't hit the radiator again and while we were working on that, the chickens in the crate on top of the cab laid eggs that rolled down the windshield, fell into the engine compartment, and broke as we were working. That created another problem. To get at an old rag to clean up the mess, we took the seat out of the truck cab and set the cardboard box out on the ground. That damn cat escaped from the box and took off. We called and hunted and finally gave up and left the cat. It was well into the afternoon before we were on our way again. Down the road we could smell eggs cooking but we just ignored it, as hungry as we were. We arrived in Yellow Pine, a small village consisting of a store, post office, and a gas station combined with a restaurant and six cabins for rent. The cabins had two beds and a sheepherder's stove with plenty of wood stacked nearby. We started a fire in the stove, spread our blankets from our bedroll out to dry, and heated some water to wash our hands and faces. Then we went next door to the restaurant to eat. After smelling burnt eggs all afternoon, ham and eggs weren't considered, so T-bone steaks were our choice at 50 cents a plate. After dinner we went back to the cabin and to bed. I was almost asleep before we got there. Morning came too soon, but we got up anyhow. We had breakfast at the restaurant by six o'clock, topped off our gas tanks at seven when the store opened, and were on our way.

The going was slow, as the road was rough. There were no bridges so we forded the streams. The streams were low so crossing wasn't a problem. At one place, the canyon narrowed so much that we had to drive in the stream for a half mile or so. We got to Big Creek headquarters about four o'clock in the afternoon. Dad went into the resort to rent a cabin and to order some supper. The resort was fairly new and very rustic—built out of logs—but small. It had one big dining room, a kitchen, a lounge, another room or two, and several new log cabins. We could get supper, but the cabins were all rented to Hollywood's Wallace Berry and his hunting entourage, although they weren't there. They were in a hunting camp down the river. We did have a nice roast beef supper. Before we ate I asked the lady where I could wash up and she handed me a small bucket of hot water and directed me to the uncovered back porch. I opened the door and saw a bear. I slammed the door shut and told the lady about the bear. She grabbed a broom and chased him away. I did a hurry-up job of washing, keeping a look out. I left a lot of dirt on the towel.

Below the buildings of the resort, the widening canyon accommodated an airstrip and quite a large meadow where the owner pastured his horses. They were used by the customers who packed into the wilderness area. It was lush enough to cut some wild hay.

We slept under the stars again. We thought about sleeping under the truck bed but a pile of hay a few yards from the truck looked mighty inviting and as the sky was clear we chose the hay. It was a comfortable bed so we went right to sleep and slept all night. The weather changed sometime during the night and we awoke in the early morning to two inches of snow. I kept nice and dry except the top of my head, which was soaking wet. It was about seven o'clock when we got up, rolled up our bed-roll, and went into the lodge for a breakfast of sourdough pancakes, syrup, and coffee and we were on our way home. We got to Yellow Pine before noon and decided to get a few snacks at the store, hoping to get to Stanley for supper. That was not to be. A few miles past Landmark Ranger Station, going toward Deadwood Summit, the steering knuckle on Dad's truck broke. It's hard to drive when the steering wheel is not connected to the front wheels. Even baling wire couldn't fix that. It needed to be taken off and a new part found—which was unlikely—or, it would have to be welded. The nearest welding shop was in Cascade, about 40 miles away. Matters were complicated by the fact that we promised Otto Centurous that we would load his cattle on Sunday to go to Ogden. And, this was Saturday. We decided to take the part off and have it welded. We would take Dad back to Warm Lake Resort and see what could be done. To get there we had to back track to the Landmark Ranger Station and go over a major summit to Warm Lake. We arrived at the resort well after dark. We decided that Dad would stay there the rest of the night and catch the mail stage into Cascade, have the knuckle welded, and get back to the truck the best he could. Geryl and I would drive to Stanley that night and be there to load the cattle the next day. But first we needed something to eat. Because it was off-season for this resort, the lady in charge said she could find us something, and she did—cold hard-boiled eggs, cold ham, and hot coffee. We ate it and Geryl and I arrived in Stanley about four a.m. We got the proprietor of the Stanley Hotel up to let us have a room and slept until nine o'clock that morning, then had more sourdough hotcakes (that was okay with me). We had a truck coming to Sunbeam and Geryl would catch a ride to Mackay. I would go on to the Centurous place and load cattle.

When I arrived at Otto's, his cattle were all ready to load. We got them all in the truck but one. It took us an hour to persuade her to go to Ogden. There always seems to be one stubborn critter in the bunch. Otto and I left his ranch on Peach Creek about one o'clock that afternoon. The best route was 15 miles to Stanley, then over Galena Summit. The old road in those days had 17 switch backs on the Salmon River side to the top of the 8,000-foot summit, and 21 switch backs down the Wood River side through Ketchum, Hailey, and Twin Falls, to Delco, where we stopped to eat supper at eleven p.m. We continued on to Utah through Snowville, Tremonton, and Brigham City to Ogden. We arrived at the stockyards about nine a.m. and unloaded the cattle. The critter that was so hard to get in the truck now didn't want to get out. I warned the stockyard employees that when she came out of the truck they had better watch out because she attacks anyone she sees. They didn't heed my warning. When she did come out, those employees were going over that high board fence like popcorn. They tried to get her into a pen. That didn't work and she came back. One of the employees had closed the gate behind the truck and I was putting the end gate up when she jumped over the gate. Then it was my turn to move and move I did. She ran out of the stockyard complex, into the street, and over the viaduct into downtown Ogden. That's when the drugstore cowboys sprang into action. They got on their steeds, pistols on their sides, lariats twirling, and went after that terrified cow that was out of her environment. I was now starting to feel sorry for her. I never found out how they got her back to the stockyard, but they did. She sold right along with the rest of Otto's cattle. Otto decided to stay down in Ogden for a few days so I was alone going home. I stopped in Roy on the way.

About ten miles from Ketchum was a very popular warm water outdoor swimming pool called Easley Hot Springs. Several churches in the area, including churches from Lost River, Shoshone, and Twin Falls held their summer church camps there. That's where Helene Tschanz, my future wife, attended camp.

Winter Ordeal

Winter had arrived and the weather was cold. I had been hauling livestock feed mainly from railcars in Mackay to wherever the ranchers were wintering their livestock. I remember I was taking one particular load into the Pahsimeroi and the truck's rear end went out at Chilly. I finally made it into a farmer's yard so I could use a phone to call home for someone to come and get me. While I was waiting, I got my tools out and removed the ring gear and pinion assembly so, when help arrived, we could take it home with us and repair it in the shop where it was warm. Dad was the help that arrived. We loaded the damaged parts in his truck and went home. After inspecting the parts, it was apparent that the oil had congealed in the below-zero weather and was unable to circulate causing the parts to fail for lack of lubrication. I had to replace the ring gear and pinion, all of the bearings and adjust all clearances so all was ready to install in the truck. Morning dawned bright and clear but it was still dark at seven o'clock. The stars were shining brightly and it was 35 degrees below zero. On the way to our disabled truck I had so many clothes on that it was an effort to move. We were taking along the thinnest rear-end oil we could get, but it was still too thick. So, we thinned it with engine oil and kerosene. Getting under that truck that frigid morning was miserable and working with mittens was somewhat trying. We used one of our fire pots under the engine while we were working and another nearby to warm our hands. We finally got the job done and were ready to go. The engine was reluctant to start because the two transmissions were so stiff, even with the thinned oil; it almost stalled the engine to get them going. When we were ready to go, I shifted into a low, forward gear and "whoops"—it went backward. Only one thing could make it do that. The ring gear and pinion assembly was upside down. That meant we had three low speeds forward and twelve speeds backward but we weren't about to change it out there. I thought of backing it the 15 miles to Mackay, but that wasn't practical, so we towed it in with the other truck. Was I ever glad to get in out of the cold. We straightened things out that afternoon and I finally delivered the load of cottonseed cake the next day.

A week later I was coming from Challis with a load of cattle that Dad was to take on to Ogden from Mackay. We had loaded the cattle at five a.m. about 20 miles from Mackay. I noticed smoke coming out of the rear of the semi-trailer. I stopped and found the outside tire on the right rear wheel was on fire. I had no way to put it out but the inside tire was holding, probably because it was another below-zero morning. I drove slowly, hoping to make it to Mackay. That time I was lucky. We put new tires on the trailer and Dad was on his way to Ogden. Trucking during the winter was a challenge.

About the middle of December, we needed another truck. The agency we dealt with in Blackfoot, which was no longer a Dodge agency, had a 1936 Ford truck on the lot. It was blue, had a very short 101-inch wheelbase, cab over, with an 85-horsepower engine. It was just what was needed to pull the green semi-van instead of that under-powered International. So, we traded it in on the new Ford that proved to be satisfactory.

The CCC contract was working better than the previous year. We were being paid on time and the new truck was making the trips faster. The second truck was the 1932 Model B with a six-foot rack covered with a double layer of canvas that made a sort of van out of it. Geryl ran the contract and the general freight very well.

ICC Regulation

1936 would be a very challenging year for the Lindburg Truck Line. The last session of Congress authorized the Interstate Commerce Commission to regulate all truck lines and individual truckers. This was the result of the railroad lobby complaining that trucks were taking business away from them. Their trouble was that they refused to provide the service the trucks could. Around the middle of December, we received a packet of material that explained what had to be done to obtain permits so we could keep operating. Dad left it up to me to figure it out, so I got Otto Jr. to help.

The provisions of the act were as follows: to establish our territory by getting statements from all of our customers stating the origin and the destination of each load. We also had to publish a tariff showing the commodities we hauled and what we were going to charge.

Our permit included two parts. The part we called general freight would now be known as common carrier. It included the routes we served, the tariff, and the frequency we would run the route. That part of the permit was easy. All of this information was on file with the Idaho Public Utilities Commission, except filing a tariff. Although our customers knew our rates, creating and filing a tariff meant our rates could be made public and upon inspection we could be penalized for not charging the right rates.

The other part of the permit was considered a contract hauler. The hard part of that would be to establish the territory we had been serving by getting all of the affidavits signed by all of the customers we had hauled for. They were scattered mainly in the states of Idaho and Utah. The tariff was not too hard, as we were allowed to bid on jobs; after the bidding process was complete, we would be required to file that bid amount with the Commission. We learned that they would check on us to see if we were following the terms of the contract. If not, we were penalized. For the first six months, checkups were pretty routine, but after that we didn't see or hear much from them. I guess there were so many permits throughout the United States that they didn't have enough people to check every complaint.

New Headquarters

Operating out of two places wasn't working well, so we were looking around for a central location. The old Mackay Livery Stable was a huge old building that was located right in the middle of town. The only occupant was a mechanic who used the rear third of the building. The walls of the building were hollow brick. The front had two large, high doors, a big window, and an entry door to what was the office. All of this was wood, as was the roof and inside partitions. The floor was concrete except for 30 feet of gravel extending back of the two large doors. These doors were about 18 feet wide and 14 feet high, and they could accommodate two trucks backed in side-by-side. With a little work, we thought it suited our situation very well. It didn't take long to find the owners. They were two brothers who had taken the building on a bad debt and were eager to sell. A deal was made, and we were the owners of the old historic building.

To make the inside of the building usable, the first thing we did was clean up and put paneling in the office. The only paneling available in those days was white pine that could be stained any shade that was wanted. A tack room that was connected to the office by a door was fixed up for storage. A bed was installed so a person or two could sleep if needed. Also, there was a connecting door from the office to the main part of the building. We had an L-shaped counter built in and a new coal-circulating heating stove put in. In the main building, we built a dock so the trucks could back in through the big doors to unload or load. Aside from the dock, the building would accommodate about three single trucks behind the office and another one or a car beside the office. We made a deal with the mechanic who occupied the back that we would not charge rent if we could work on our trucks back there. We would pay him for any time he spent helping us maintain our trucks. Our office was well equipped with a file cabinet, a big desk, a typewriter, and an adding machine. We made good use of that place in the coming months.

Another Winter

1935 had been a good year for us and it was about over. It seemed like everyone was getting ready for Christmas but us. We were so busy that time just slipped by. Geryl was the exception. He managed his work and Christmas very well. He was a great organizer. We had our Christmas Eve and our dinner at Darlington that year. As I remember, that was the last Christmas I spent at home. There was quite a lot of snow in the valley and surrounding mountains. I don't remember who was running the milk route during the holidays, but I helped with the CCC contract. I took the runs from Pocatello to Paul and Rock Creek, and from Pocatello to Logan, Utah. I went on down for a load of four-inch balls for the ore mill at the Ima Mines at Patterson. I got back to Mackay about noon on New Year's Eve. Geryl arrived about the same time; he followed me with the semi load of CCC freight for the camps down Salmon City way. It sure was nice to get the trucks inside of our new terminal.

Otto Jr. was in the new office trying to figure out the tariffs that had to be filed by July. We had subscribed to the general tariff that only applied to us when we picked up freight from a connecting carrier that was to be delivered to some town on our route. They furnished the bill of lading and then we had to look up the rate in the general tariff and make out the freight bills. Then, at the end of the month, we settled with the connecting carriers, depending on the origin and destination of each shipment. We had connecting arrangements with three common carriers.

January was generally slow, especially that year because we had a lot of snow in the Lost River and Upper Salmon. The road contractors just about shut down for the month, along with the mining operations. The exceptions were Clayton Silver and the Ima Tungsten Mines at Patterson. They would need a load of supplies once in a while. And, maybe a load or two of livestock went to Ogden. Hogs generally moved well that time of the year. Hogs were nice to haul. We bedded them with quite a lot of straw; they would really snuggle down in straw to keep warm. If the pig on the outside started to get cold, it would climb on top of the pile and root his way into the center. There would be a lot of loud complaining and then it was quiet again. We always kept the front of the stock rack covered with canvas to keep the cold air off livestock in cold weather.

In those days there wasn't much going on the Yankee Fork, although some folks lived there year round. The mode of travel was by skis or snowshoes. Some of them would come down to the Sunbeam Store for their mail and supplies that they could carry. That was quite a hike. Bonanza was about 14 miles away and Custer about 16. Some of the old miners would spend their time highgrading the old mines. And, some made good money the following fall when they shipped the ore that they spent the winter digging out. The road up the main Salmon was kept open all winter long as far as Stanley and toward Galena Summit as far as Obsidian. The road was closed from there on over the summit and down the Wood River side. The CCC contract, milk route, and common carrier routes were steady.

I might add here that Otto Jr. and I worked a lot at the office and most of the time late into the night. Before we had sleeping quarters fixed up in our terminal, I would stay at Tschanzes' at night and sometimes have meals there instead of going down to Darlington. Otto was doing most of the office work. Most of the billing would have to be done whenever the loaded trucks would come in. Most of the billing was for the common carrier trucks. They would be loaded with shipments for several shippers. The drivers would have documents called bills of lading that listed the customer's name, what the shipment contained, origin, destination, shipper's name, and shipper's address. They contained everything but the rates. The person doing the billing had to apply the rating. Often the truck would have shipments for different destinations and often the truck wouldn't be going to all those places, so some shipments would have to be taken off and left on the dock or transferred to a truck that delivered to those destinations. The freight for Mackay was taken off for delivery the next morning.

The last part of February things began to stir in the Upper Salmon country. Some men were interested in the old mining dumps—to see if they contained enough value to work again. When the mines were running back at the turn of the century, the methods of recovering the minerals from the ore weren't efficient, so a lot of the valuable minerals went in the dumps. As the Depression continued, men looking for some way to make a buck were interested in the old mining dumps. Several samples were assayed to determine what would pay to rework. By the end of March there was still a lot of snow left, but some men were impatient enough to walk or snowshoe into some of the old mines. They packed enough provisions and bedrolls so they could stay two or three days and collect samples.

Tariff Negotiations

Near the end of March, I was approached by Jess Jarvis, the manager of Challis Transportation Company. They were also applying for permits from Mackay to all points on the Salmon River above the mouth of Pahsimeroi up to Stanley. Jarvis asked if we would be interested in filing a joint tariff. I told him that sounded good to me and that I would let him know after talking with Dad. He also mentioned that the Benedict Truck Lines that operated from Pocatello to Salmon City was applying for a common carrier permit from Pocatello to Salmon City and all points in between. Benedict also would be interested in filing a joint tariff. After talking with Dad and Geryl, we decided that it would be a good thing for us and all concerned because it would make us equal as far as rates were concerned. We informed the other two that it was satisfactory with us. Our services seldom overlapped anyway.

The first tariff meeting with these two carriers was set in Salmon City to start at nine a.m. on a Monday morning. Dad thought both Otto Jr. and I should go. The first order of business was to appoint a secretary. We chose Otto Jr. and that turned out to be a good choice. Our discussions centered on all the places we had served between Pocatello, Blackfoot, and Salmon City, and up the river to Stanley. A list was made of all the places we served starting with Midway, which was the first place we served out of Pocatello. It was just a service station but they handled a few groceries, pop, and beer. We were the only one that served Midway, so listing commodities and setting the rates was easy because we were satisfied with what we were already charging. Arco was next, then Moore, Darlington and Leslie. Those were quite easy because we were the only one serving those places, too. Mackay was different because it was served by both Challis Transportation and Lindburg Truck Line. It was also our headquarters so it took the most time.

About six o'clock we took time out for supper, then came back and finished the tariff for Mackay. We adjourned about nine p.m. until nine a.m. the following Thursday. That gave Otto time to type his notes and organize them to show what our final product would look like. In the meantime, I installed a short block in one of the Fords—an engine block containing all the moving parts of the engine, but not the oil pan, the heads, water pump, fan, distributor, and so forth. Thursday arrived and Otto Jr. and I left early for Salmon City so he could get his papers organized for the presentation.

The first order of business was to review what we had accomplished at the previous meeting. Otto Jr. passed a copy of his papers to each of us. The other two members were surprised by the finished product and indicated their approval. We worked all day on the rest of the tariff and still didn't finish, so we agreed to come back on Saturday. That gave Otto Jr. Friday to organize the previous day's work. He worked all day and into the night. By Saturday morning we were ready to go again and were finished by early afternoon. We spent some time reviewing what we had done and then left it up to Otto Jr. to put it in final form. We had decided to meet in Mackay after the two other shippers received the final form. However, that meeting never took place. As soon as they received the final product they phoned their approval and asked Otto to have the local printer print ten copies for each of them and bill them for their share. Within a week we had our finished tariff ready to file with the ICC.

ICC Operating Permit

Now we had to get our affidavits in order to establish the boundaries for our operating permits. Our drivers were very good about getting affidavits signed from the ones they contacted and all that we mailed were returned signed. Our farthest point south was Kanab, Utah, almost at the Arizona border, and the farthest point north was Cocolalla, Idaho, just a few miles south of Sandpoint. Otto Jr. spent the next week getting everything in order to send to the ICC, and we mailed it all to their office in Ogden, Utah, by the first of June. I had carried an old box camera in the truck and took pictures of nearly all of the places I went. We sent the photos along hoping they would help our cause.

Days went by with no word from the ICC. Then on the very last day, we received a letter informing us we could keep operating pending a hearing at nine a.m. on July 14 in their office in the Capitol building in Boise, Idaho. That bothered us some, so we fretted until the hearing. Otto Jr. was especially worried as he had reviewed all of the documents that were sent in and said everything was in order as far as he could tell.

As the day of the hearing approached, Otto Jr. thought Dad should go along, but he declined, so Otto Jr. and I were on our own. We went to Boise the afternoon before the hearing. The next morning a couple of nervous young kids, maybe in their early twenties, entered the hearing room to find three commissioners—probably fifteen or more years our senior—and their secretary. To our surprise they stood up to shake hands with us. I think they were surprised that we were as young as we were. That surely eased the tension as far as we were concerned. The first question they asked was "who owned the Lindburg Truck Line?" It seemed we had failed to fill out that part of the application. The answer was Mr. C.B. Lindburg. Then, "what were our positions?" The answer was that I was his son and helped with management, along with three younger brothers. The next question kind of threw me for a loop. Otto Jr. was considered an employee, but to my thinking that wasn't doing him justice. So, after a slight hesitation, I answered "Office Manager." They commented on how complete our application was and then adjourned the meeting until one p.m. When we returned, they handed us our temporary permit. We were given all of Idaho and Utah to haul livestock, salt, mining machinery and supplies, ore, ore concentrates, cattle feed, lumber, cement, and building supplies. We could pass through Montana on Highway 93 to haul ore to north Idaho and lumber and shingles back. But, we were denied service to points in Montana. Our common carrier permit remained the same as we filed, which was the same as our Idaho PUC permit. The ICC accepted our common carrier tariff so we got practically everything we filed for. The only other requirement was that the Commission would inspect our trucks every once in a while to ensure that they were in safe running condition—brakes, running lights, etc. We felt that we were set to operate legally.

The Sun Valley Stage Lines were not as lucky as we were. Although their route was approved, their tariff was unacceptable. Somehow they learned that Otto Jr. had experience along that line, so they wasted no time asking for his help. I don't remember where their meeting was held; probably Twin Falls, where their main office was located at the south end of their operation. They served every town between Twin Falls and Ketchum and Sun Valley. Otto Jr. was gone a couple of days and I guess he got the job done. Sixty-some[7] years later, Sun Valley Stages are still operating.

Moving the Shovel

A mining company up Stanley Creek in the Stanley Basin was exploring their leased ground, so they bought a half-yard

---

[7] Sun Valley Stages has since ceased operations

bucket shovel from the Shoshone Irrigation District. Today, a shovel of that nature is called a dragline. The only difference is a dragline drags the bucket toward the machine to load itself, whereas a shovel loads its bucket by pushing away from the machine. A shovel works better on a hillside. This machinery weighed in excess of 25 tons. So that meant it had to be taken apart before it could be moved.

We went down to move it early on a hot summer day. The first thing we did was start it up and place the boom and slide bar and bucket on the truck that Dad was driving. Then we unhooked the cables and power wound them on the drums that are located in the cab. Then we unbolted the boom from the cab and crawler tracks on which it moved itself. The next thing we did was remove the cab. That contained the engine controls and winches that the cables were wound on. The weight was a little over ten tons. All that had to be done by hand. We had four jacks—one on each corner. We jacked a little at a time and then put a timber under the raised area. We also built timbers to set the jacks, added a timber under the jacks, and kept repeating that process until we had the cab lifted free of the tracks. Then we pulled the tracks out from under the cab with the other truck. It was high enough so we could back in the truck that was to haul the cab. Then we let it down a little bit at a time until the truck had its load. It was heavy.

At about three in the afternoon we were loaded and ready to go. We were coming back for the tracks the next day—or so we thought. The day was a scorcher; more than 100 degrees out in the desert, where we were working. The only water we had was in our water bags. The fellow from the irrigation district who was helping us decided about noon to go and bring us lunch, and especially drinks. He brought beer. Now, neither of us drank beer, but we drank that. As a matter of fact, that was the only time I ever saw my Dad drink an alcoholic beverage.

We started for Stanley in the middle of the afternoon. We didn't like to travel in the heat but anything was better than sitting around in that heat, even if we had trouble keeping the trucks cool. We arrived in Ketchum about 7:30 p.m. and decided to stay overnight. We were really bushed.

At the time, Idaho had wide-open gambling. We got a room in the St. George Hotel, where the management had converted the whole lower floor for gambling tables and a bar. The upper floor had rooms that they rented out. I was so tired I went right to bed. Dad thought he'd go down and watch the gambling for a while. He said that he had watched for a while and noticed the black numbers were coming up most of the time, so he put a dollar on a black number and sure enough, black came up. It paid $60. He put the money in his pocket, came right upstairs, and went to bed. Later Dad said when the dealer paid him the $60 he was very put out that Dad didn't play some more so he (the dealer) could try to get the money back. But, Dad left anyway. I think that was the profit for that trip.

We were up about five the next morning. We had breakfast at an all-night greasy spoon and continued on to Stanley. We had a good head wind that kept the truck engine cool. But the going was slow: because of the steady climb from Ketchum to the foot of Galena Summit, the 21 switchbacks to the top on a single-track road, and the 17 switchbacks on the other side of the hill down to river grade. The new road was fairly level for the next ten miles on to Stanley. The last five or six miles were very primitive. We got there too late to unload but we did talk them into unloading the boom and the rest of the stuff from Dad's truck so we could go back to Stanley for the night. After a breakfast of sourdough hotcakes we went back to the mine to unload the shovel cab. When we got there, the mine crew had all of the timbers needed to set the cab on and had started to jack the cab off of the truck. In an hour we were unloaded and headed back to Stanley. We left Dad's truck there and both of us got in my truck and headed to the Shoshone Desert to get the shovel tracks. We got there about three in the afternoon. The irrigation company employees had their Cat out there, had dozed a ramp, and were waiting for us so they could pull the tracks onto the truck. The tracks were about a foot wider than the bed of the truck so they stuck out six inches on each side. After chaining and blocking the load so it couldn't move, we left for Stanley. We arrived in Ketchum at 7:30 p.m. and had our supper at the same old greasy spoon; it was the only restaurant in Ketchum at that time. We decided it was too early to stop and, considering that there was two of us to drive, we continued on. The truck ran cooler and better at night. Dad said he would drive so I could rest. I had no problem sleeping in a truck cab and got a pretty good rest by the time we got to the foot of Galena Summit. The switchbacks to the top of the summit made it a long grind. I had to shift gears so often it really kept me on my toes. If I missed a gear it was doubtful that the brakes would keep us from rolling backward. We reached the summit as it was breaking day. We still had to go down the switchbacks. Holding the load back in the low gears was a slow process. After we got to the bottom of the hill, Dad drove on to Stanley. I slept and we arrived in Stanley at nine the next morning. We had been on the road more than 12 hours since we had left Ketchum. We had breakfast in Stanley and arrived at the mine around noon. They were ready for us when we got there, so it didn't take long to unload. They just pulled the tracks off with a Caterpillar tractor.

Back at Stanley we met Geryl as he was delivering freight. He informed us that the men at the Sunbeam Mine who had been reworking the old dump had called and said they had a railcar load of ore ready to ship. That was the reason he was driving a flatbed truck—so that he could take a load of ore back. He had planned to take the sideboards off and put on the low

Unloading ore—Dad (center)

boards that he had with him. The ore is heavy so the sideboards we used for that were only 16 inches high. Dad's truck was ready to haul ore but my truck just had the flat platform. So I stopped at a sawmill and got some 16-foot planks and stakes. It didn't take long to fashion a makeshift setup so I could haul a load of ore. The mine had built an ore bin so we loaded by driving under the bin, opening the chute, and letting the ore run onto the truck. When you had enough on the front, it was your guess when you had a load. We had all three trucks loaded by six o'clock. The three of us had about three-quarters of a railcar load. We arrived in Mackay at eleven p.m. Dad and I were bushed. We hadn't had our clothes off for more than 48 hours. We all rode home to Darlington in a new 1936 Plymouth we had recently bought. We were up the next morning and back to Mackay to unload the ore. Dad and I had all three trucks to unload. A load of supplies had come in the night before and Geryl had to take it to the CCC camps in the Salmon City area. Otto Jr. hadn't come to work yet, but we had the manifests and freight bills made out and on the seat. We decided we would unload Dad's truck first so he could go back up for the load that would finish loading the railcar. That left the other two trucks for me to unload. They had to be unloaded by hand, and the ore shoved over the side of the open gondola railcar. Although the trucks had steel floors, it was still a laborious job. I was about half unloaded when a fellow came along and asked if I needed help. I said sure. He soon returned with a shovel and we made short work of unloading that truck.

The fellow who helped me was a fixture around Mackay. I know his last name was Allen but I never heard him ever called by anything but Smut Allen. Although he was always well shaved and had a clean face and hands, I don't think he ever washed his clothes. He'd wear his bib overalls until they got so dirty and filthy that he couldn't stand them. About once a month he'd blossom out in a new shirt and overalls. I have heard that he was a World War I disabled veteran. I had never known him to have a steady job, just odd jobs here and there. He lived with his brother who I never knew to work at all. They were bachelors and lived just across the alley from the place where my sister, Edythe, lives now. I never knew them to spend a dime on anything such as meals, liquor, or any other luxury, although they hung around the pool hall a lot and watched the gambling during the day. But seldom after dark.

I owed him for helping me that day. He said he would like to unload the ore trucks as they came in and would want a dollar a truckload. We offered him 25 cents a ton, and because most of the time we loaded more than five tons, he seemed pleased. We always weighed every load anyway because we were paid by weight. He didn't drive so someone had to drive to the rail siding and spot the trucks for him and then go get the trucks when he had them unloaded. You could count on him being there whenever a truckload of ore came in—night or day.

My next job was hauling lambs into the railhead at
Ketchum for the Kimball Sheep Company, which was on the
Wood River. That took Dad and me about three, eighteen-hour
days. We were surprised to see how much building was going
on at Sun Valley.

Building Sun Valley

The Union Pacific Railroad searched all over the West for
a place to build a ski resort. A fellow named Harriman[8] was
president of the company at the time. There were two criteria:
it had to be served by Union Pacific, and it had to have a long
snow season. Ketchum had both. So, they bought a ranch on
Trail Creek next to the town of Ketchum. As I remember, the
rancher's name was Hays. The rail company paid what most
people thought was an outlandish sum of $40,000 for his 120
acres, a house, a nice red barn, and some out buildings. The old
red barn still stands at its old location. Mr. Hays took the
$40,000 and bought a feed lot in the Twin Falls area. When we
were there about the middle of August, the big lodge was about
complete; the skating rink was nearly finished; and they were
landscaping that area to the north, where the Opera House was
being built. Across the street from the Opera House, the Challenger Inn was under construction and right next to it, also under construction, was the bicycle shop—which was then the ski
shop. That part of the building was built over the road. On the
end of the building was a heated pool with the sides all glassed
in and open at the top. To the west of the Challenger Inn there
were several small shops which included space for a post office.
The street was narrow and wouldn't accommodate autos. I

[8] William Averell Harriman was a businessman, politician, and diplomat. He was
the son of railroad baron E. H. Harriman.

guess it was for maintenance vehicles—golf carts and the like. From the Challenger Inn there was just a pathway in front of the Opera House connecting it to the main lodge's ice rink complex. They were also building a ski lift on Dollar Mountain, said to be the first ski lift in the world. It was designed and built by the Union Pacific engineers.

There were a lot of men working—a lot of locals and a lot of every craft. I guess the men who were from outside the area all lived in a work train and must have had families living with them. There were so many railcars that they took up two sidings. Most of the landscaping was done with horses. It sure was a boom time for Ketchum and Hailey. Opening date was set for December 21, 1936. It looked like a lot of work had to be done before then. It was an open fall. They worked right up to opening day and still had no snow.

Moving a Railroad Diner

There was a family that lived about a mile above Mackay, and on their place was a large grove of cottonwood trees. They were building a large outdoor dance pavilion right in the center of that grove of trees. They bought an old railroad dining car for a concession stand that was to be located on one side bordered by the highway. The end of the rail line was at Mackay and the dining car somehow had to be moved to their property, about a mile. Guess who said we'd move it? Dad! It looked impossible to me but he said we'd move it, so we did. It came in without wheels under it and was sitting on a flat car in Mackay. It was much too long for anything we had to haul it on, so we had to figure a way to get it moved. Dad, Otto Jr., and I worked with planks, rollers, and bars and finally got one end of the diner car loaded onto our biggest truck. It was a long way to the other end. Using the same procedure with planks, rollers, and bars, we loaded the other end on the second truck. That truck would have to travel backwards. We had a 12x12 between the truck beds and the bottom of the rail car so that the car would not slide and to provide a little leeway for movement.[9] Anything that resembled a sharp turn was ruled out because it was so wide it took up most of the highway. We notified the State Patrol and a patrolman came down to look at it. I don't think he believed what he saw. He wanted us to pull it away from the track to see how it was going to ride. I was to drive the front truck that was doing the pulling. Dad was in the truck that was to go backward. He was to just leave it in neutral and let it free wheel. I started my truck, put it in its lowest gear, let up on the clutch easy, and everything began to move. I made an easy turn to line it up with Main Street and everything went fine. We decided to wait until daybreak to go onto the highway because there would be less traffic.

Daybreak came and we were ready. I started my truck and we began to move. We thought if we could make the turn onto the highway everything after that would be all right—it was a straight road the rest of the way. Because there were no cars on Main Street that early, I stayed on the left side of Main Street and before I reached the highway, I started to make my right turn to the left side of the highway. I executed the turn perfectly. It took about a block to straighten out and we were on our way. We didn't travel very fast. It took us more than a half-hour to go the mile before we left the highway onto the site where we were to unload. The owner had dozed a level grade down to the spot where he wanted the dining car unloaded. He even had the timbers that the railcar would rest on. Otto Jr. followed us with the timbers we needed to unload. Before noon

---

[9] There is a photo of this load in the Mackay Museum, Mackay, Idaho.

we were unloaded and the job was done. I thought at the time that if we have another job like that, I would be an old man.

We spent the rest of the summer and fall hauling cattle. We also hauled ore from the old mines that were being worked over, making trips to Utah with cattle and, often, with high-grade ore. The cattle trucks back-hauled fruit and melons, and the ore trucks back-hauled supplies for the mines that were operating. Otherwise, fall was pretty routine. We kept very busy and winter came too soon.

One interesting event was a trip to Park City, Utah, for a load of coal. Although the railroad rate was so cheap that we couldn't compete, we would back-haul a load for ourselves once in a while. A 3-inch by 8-inch chunk of coal was the very best, and cost $3.85 a ton at the mine. We were so busy working that getting wood wasn't practical anymore; so we burned coal.

Sun Valley Opening

Winter was upon us and the opening of Sun Valley Resort was scheduled for the first day of winter: December 21. The year was 1936. It promised to be a gala event and anyone who wished to attend was invited. So, I think it was Hilmer, a couple of the McAffee boys, and I, decided to go over to witness the event. It was an open winter so far—no snow on the Lost River side, so we decided to go over Trail Creek Summit. It was quite rough on the Lost River side, but on the Sun Valley side a new road had been constructed from the top of the summit along the hillside. The dugway was nice and two lanes wide, although it was still gravel. It was graded very smoothly. We were driving a new Plymouth. It had a heater, but in those days the heaters in cars weren't very effective so we wore plenty of warm clothes. And in cold weather, it was a chore to keep the frost off of the

119

inside of the windows and windshield. There were several devices on the market that were supposed to keep frost off the windshield, but the most effective was one made of glass that was held tightly against the windshield by rubber suction cups, forming a seal. It had heating elements and connected to the car's electrical system, but vision was still limited because the device was only a foot long and six inches wide.

We arrived at the resort about two in the afternoon and the first thing we did was try to find a place to stay the night. Every available room was already taken. Next, we looked for something to eat. We didn't try the main lodge—it looked too high-toned for us—but the Challenger Inn had a restaurant, buffet style. We got all we wanted to eat there for 75 cents a plate.

The Union Pacific ran a special train full of very popular people they had invited; a lot of movie stars and some industrialists. The train was supposed to be met by sleighs pulled by horses all decked out with sleigh bells. Because there was no snow, buses met the train and the passengers were bused to the lodge. I think the trainload of notables were guests of the railroad company. Some of the movie stars we recognized; most of them we didn't. Some that we did recognize were Robert Young, Myrna Loy, Gary Cooper, Red Skelton, Ann Southern, Roy Rogers, and probably others that I don't remember. There were people everywhere. The railroad folks were showing off all of their facilities. Guests were bused out to the new ski lift and people rode up to the top of Dollar Mountain and back down. (They either had to ride the lift down or walk because there was no snow for skiing.) There was a building up at the top where coffee and pastries were available. We never tried to ride it because there were so many people ahead of us.

The whole Sun Valley complex was lit up in the Christmas spirit with colored lights everywhere. In those days, the colored lights were regular bulbs with lower wattage. They were small, like a fifteen-watt bulb. Although on the Christmas trees inside of the buildings, fancy, glass, low-watt, pear-shaped bulbs were used. There were Christmas trees and decorations everywhere.

As the sun went behind the mountain, the evening cold set in and people began to move inside, except the folks on the skating rink. That was a very popular place. It was full of people skating all afternoon and evening. It was really decorated. Everyone was trying to find a place to eat. The dining room at the main lodge was full of the guests of the Union Pacific and so was the bar. The veranda wasn't very popular that night because of the cold. We stood in line and finally ate at the Challenger Inn again. The food was good and the prices were reasonable. There were a few people using the warm-water glassed-in roofless pools at both the main lodge and at the end of the ski assembly building. Entertainment was beginning in the dining room and in the auditorium in the main lodge, the Opera House, the dining room of the Challenger Inn, and the ski assembly room. That's where we spent the evening listening to and watching Red Skelton. That was an evening full of laughs; the best I ever saw him perform. The room was packed and he went on until midnight. It may be well to note that Sun Valley had hired a professional skier from Norway as an instructor and exhibition skier. He didn't have much to do on opening day but get acquainted. I think he became naturalized because he was a resident of Ketchum when I left in 1943.

It was past midnight and time for us to head home. But first we toured the gambling joints in Ketchum. (To my knowledge, Sun Valley had no gambling joints.) They were going full blast. We saw nothing interesting there so we left. The night was clear and cold. Still no snow, so we went over Trail Creek Summit and arrived home a little after three in the morning.

On December 23, two days after the grand opening, the weather changed and Sun Valley got more than two feet of the light powdery snow—the kind they are famous for.

Winter Again

1936 was quite an exciting year that ended with a lot of snow in those last few days. We had a white Christmas. Because of the snow, the rest of the year was pretty slow. And the highway crews were slow in clearing the roads.

The New Year came without more snow, but the snow from the last storm had settled so there was only about a foot on the ground. We had a little trouble running the general freight route and the CCC contract because of the snow. Although the road across the Arco Desert was usually open, the wind would often close it and those who were traveling on it would be stuck until the snowplow would come to their rescue. Our trucks were stalled there once in a while. A lot of the folks who stalled suffered the cold because they rarely had adequate, warm clothing with them. We always tried to prepare for such emergencies.

I remember I went to Inkom one late afternoon that winter. I didn't stop in Pocatello because of the weather, but I did stop in Blackfoot at a coffee shop where a number of trucks stopped—to see if I could find out how the weather was across the desert to Arco. I talked to a driver who had just come from Arco and he said it was snowing lightly and that I should have no trouble. So I drank a cup of coffee and left for Arco. Starting out wasn't bad, but the further I got, the harder it snowed. A couple of miles before I got to Midway a strong northeast wind was blowing so much snow that I could hardly see the road. I came to a cut where the road was lower than either side and it was full of snow. I nearly got through, but suddenly I was stuck.

The wind was howling, the snow was blowing, and it was very cold. I could walk to Midway but, in a blinding storm like this, I might get lost. So, I decided to stay with the truck, hoping a snowplow would come and help. But that could be some time as it was 90 miles across the desert. Then an idea struck. I had a load of cement in bags and they were hot when they were loaded. They were covered with a tarp to keep them dry. So, I just got under the tarp and stayed warm and dry—in fact, a little too warm. I even got a little sleep. The wind had died down and about sunup the snowplow arrived. The wind had blown the snow around the truck, so I was really stuck. Although it had stopped snowing and blowing, the temperature dropped. The fellows on the plow soon had me out and pulled me so I could get going. I thought I might have to build a fire under the engine, but it finally started. About a mile down the road the engine began misfiring and it was losing power. I had to take it out of gear but tried to keep it running. When I opened the hood I found the whole engine compartment full of snow, so as the engine warmed up, the snow started to melt and was shorting out the wiring, spark plugs, and distributor. It took me two hours to remove enough of the snow before I started the engine again. It ran rough, but I kept it running and it finally got enough power to pull the load. Even with the warm clothes I was wearing, I was nearly frozen—especially my feet. I stopped at Midway to warm up. A lot of other people had the same idea so the little, old service station was really crowded. I drank a cup of hot coffee and was on my way.

It was about noon when I arrived in Arco. It had been 24 hours since I had anything to eat so I stopped and had breakfast: ham, eggs, hot cakes, and all the coffee I could drink. The cost? 35 cents. I got to Mackay about two p.m. and was really tired. There were 150 bags of cement to unload but I was lucky to have a lot of help, so that didn't take long. Then we unhooked the semi and pulled the truck into the shop for maintenance.

But as soon as I got warm, I got awfully sleepy. So I got a bite to eat, went to bed, and slept until sunup the next morning.

As I remember, the next two weeks were exceptionally cold so I spent most of my time inside doing maintenance on trucks—changing oil and so forth. There was always plenty to do. Geryl and Dewey took care of the general freight and the CCC commodities. They tried to do it with one truck. We felt safer with two drivers and they had all of the emergency equipment available. Too bad we didn't have cellular phones in those days. If they had trouble, they had to get word home the best they could. If they had more weight than they could haul, then Dad and I would have to take a truck and go help out. We had to take a load that they brought to Mackay on to the CCC camps down in the Salmon City Country. It wasn't as cold down there as it was in the Lost River, Wood River, and Upper Salmon countries. Two weeks later, the weather began to moderate some. Although there wasn't much ore hauling because roads to the mines were under several feet of snow, some miners would stay in their mine camps and continue working, so it looked like we would be plenty busy when things opened up in the spring.

About the first of February, we took delivery of a new Ford truck. It had a grey cab-over engine and standard wheelbase. It would take a 14-foot bed, and would be equipped for most everything but livestock. It turned out to be a real work truck.

Renting Boats

A development that I think should be noted was that Elmer Peterson and Otto Tschanz Sr. decided to go in the boat-renting business. I should explain that fishing was very good at the Mackay Reservoir but for the best fishing a boat was needed, so the successful fishermen brought their own boats. Well, Otto and Elmer decided to build twelve-foot-long boats of wood. Elmer was to build the boats and Otto would help buy the lumber and furnish the motors. During the fishing season they rented them out as fast as they could build them. They made some money all right. But they were a headache, too. A lot of the dudes who rented them couldn't start the motors so someone would have to go up to the dam, start the motors for them, and try to teach them how to do it themselves. I didn't think some of those guys would ever learn. It was the middle of the season when they finished building the boats and it seemed they were all rented out every day. Elmer and Otto didn't realize that that it would keep someone so busy renting boats and starting motors. They also found that some people are less than honest. Renters would take the motors, then claim that they came loose from the boat and fell in the lake. So, the motors had to be chained and padlocked to the boat—to keep the customer honest. The next year they built several more boats and bought motors. When Otto's sons, Mac and Boyd, got out of school in the spring, they set up camp on the lake above the dam and rented the boats and started the motors—24 hours a day. Some fishermen liked to go out on the water at daybreak, so sometimes it meant getting up at four in the morning to rent boats.

Lucky Boy Mine

There was renewed interest in the old Lucky Boy Mine by its owners. I say old mine because it was operated in the late 1800s until 1909, when it ceased operations because Custer Mill shut down. Although the mine was a quarter of a mile straight over the mountain from the Custer Mill, it was still about five miles on the other side of the mountain by road, so the ore was moved to the mill by a tramway. The road was hardly a road at all, so when the owners put a crew of miners in there to see if they could find some ore worth mining, they had the road plowed out up to the mine. It was already plowed up to Bonanza because of the CCC camp. The roads were kept open to the Wild Horse and Pass Creek CCC camps all winter. There was hardly any snow in Salmon City and the surrounding area, so the camps in that area had open road all winter. The weather was moderating and on some days even thawed a little.

It was the middle of March and the snow was leaving Arco Desert and the Lost River roads. One Saturday, Hilmer had gone to Pocatello with the semi van for supplies for the local CCC camps and I was returning from Utah with a load of salt going to Challis for the Forest Service. (The Forest Service then would take the salt by airplane and drop the bags of salt over the wilderness area to form salt licks for the wild life.) As we arrived in Mackay, Mom sent word that a Mr. Dunn from the Lucky Boy Mine was very eager to see us. He was staying at the hotel and was leaving the next morning so we had to see him as soon as possible. When we found him he said that he had several ton of high-grade ore that he wanted to send to the smelters in Utah, and some ore that wasn't so rich that would be hauled to Mackay and loaded onto railcars. The next day, a Sunday, Hilmer, another driver, and I went up the Yankee Fork to look the road over. The road left Yankee Fork at Fourth of July Creek, then went by switchback over on the Custer side, then over the hill down about a quarter mile to the mine. We could only get our car up to the end of the switchback and then had to walk the remainder of the six miles. When we got to the mine we found a crew of six men working there. They had the ore bin full of high-grade ore that could be shipped to Utah. The ore bin was built from timbers left over from the mine's early operating days. They estimated that the bin held 100 tons. We had to figure out how to get it down to the Yankee Fork Road and over the road we had just walked. In the first place, that hillside was a poor place to try to build a road. It must have been a leftover skid trail from the days when they used horses to skid logs for firewood down to the Custer Mill to fire the boilers for steam. One section of the road had a 32 percent grade and right below that was a spring that ran down the road. The two reasons that the miners couldn't get their cars to the mine were real obstacles for our trucks. The first, water from the spring was frozen on the road, and second, the steep grade. There wasn't much that could be done with the steep grade but we felt that we might be able to handle it if the road was smoothed out and the snow was removed from the rest of the road. And, of course, the ice from the spring was removed.

After talking with Mr. Dunn, he agreed to have a Caterpillar tractor and bulldozer come and work the road over. We, on the other hand, would move 20 tons of ore to Utah—if we could negotiate the steep grade. If I remember right, we were paid 25 dollars a ton. We were to start as soon as the road was cleared.

It never rains unless it pours. A few days before Mr. Dunn called to say that the road was ready, Ima Mines at Patterson had a carload of concentrates they wanted hauled. Because the road over Doublesprings was still snowed in, we had to haul from Patterson down the Pahsimeroi River to the Salmon River Road to Challis and then to Mackay. So we hired another driver. Good drivers were easy to get as there were a lot of people out of work. We hired a fellow named Jack Monarch. He made one trip with me and then took over the Patterson haul.

I helped Elmer put new brakes on the 1936 Ford truck to get it ready to try the 32 percent grade on the Lucky Boy hill. The big day arrived and we left for the Lucky Boy. We took two trucks because we decided that if we made it up the hill that we would haul a half load down, load it on the Dodge and go after another half load. As it turned out we made it up the grade with no problems and, by using the lowest gear coming down, the truck held back the half load easily. So we went after the other half load. We spun the wheels a little but we made it. With the right gear and right speed the hill could be made with no problem. The second half load came down as easily as the first. Then Dad had the idea to try a full load. The Cat skinner would come down to the top of the grade and chain the back of the truck to the Cat, to help hold the truck back. We now had two full loads to go to the smelter in Utah. We both had good back hauls. I was loaded with four tons of four-inch balls for the ball mill at the Ima, as well as four barrels of chemicals and some small cartons of nuts and bolts. Dad had 5-½ tons of ball mill liners for the Clayton Silver Mine. Then it was back to the Lucky Boy to get more ore to go to Utah. We made it up the hill to the mine without much trouble and, with the help of the Cat, we made it down with two full loads. After stopping at Mackay overnight, we were off to the smelter in Utah. The back hauls were not as good this time. I had a couple tons of mining tools for the Lucky Boy. Dad had hauled sideboards and left them in Pocatello, so when he got back to Pocatello, he hauled a load of subsistence for Paul and Rock Creek CCC camps, and then went back to Pocatello for loads to Pass Creek and Wild Horse CCC camps.

In the meantime, the Lucky Boy was building a switchback that would bypass that steep grade, making it a lot easier (they thought) for the trucks to travel up to the mine. The problem was that the switchback wasn't wide enough to get a truck around without backing up midway through the turn. Because it sloped downhill, it was hard to back up.

We first tried with an empty truck. Just as we figured, we could only get half around the turn without backing. By turning the wheels straight and backing up, and then by turning the wheels sharp right, we could complete the turn. The only problem that remained was that the turn was so steep that the brakes would not stop a loaded truck. Consequently, we knew the truck would run off the switchback and end up about a mile down the steep mountainside into the Yankee Fork adjacent to Custer. Then Dad had an idea (he was always coming up with bright ideas). He said we could make the turn by using a block of wood to block one set of back wheels and then back up, turn the front wheels sharp right, and make the turn. The block of wood was 12-by-12-by-18 inches with a Q-strap attached to remove the block when we were ready to go around the switchback. To make this work we had to travel together. We loaded two trucks with ore at the mine and I was in the lead truck when we started down the mountain. We stopped on a level place just before going down the steep grade to the switchback. Dad left his truck there and walked down to the switchback, got the block ready (boy, was I nervous), then motioned me to start down the grade. The truck had 12 speeds forward. I selected the lowest gear so it just crawled along. I tried to stop with the brakes but no way would they stop that truck. There was no turning back. The only thing that would stop me from going over the switchback down that steep mountain into the river was Dad and that block of wood. I started making the turn. I was standing on the brakes but kept going and going. I couldn't see the road in front of me anymore and thought I was going over the side. Suddenly, the truck came to a stop. The block of wood worked. Then, racing the motor, I shifted into reverse and backed up as far as the bank would let me. Dad moved the block of wood, which held the truck while I shifted into forward gear. Then he removed it and I turned the front wheels sharp right and made it around the rest of the bend just as planned. We went through the same procedure with his truck only I handled the block. Dad and I hauled several loads of ore around that switchback.

The snow was about gone and we were getting real busy with the folks at the Silver King and the Buckskin mines. Then, to top it off, the Lucky Boy notified us that they intended to install an ore mill because of all of the low-grade ore they had discovered. The machinery would come from Boise where one of the men involved in the mine, a fellow named Burroughs (some relation to the people that made the adding machine), also owned a new and used mining machinery business. The machinery was coming from his yards. That meant we would have to amend our tariff to accommodate that business. As the general tariff was way out of line, we would have to include heavy mining machinery, explosives, and chemicals. No one showed up to contest our amended tariff rates at the hearing the Interstate Commerce Commission held, so we were free to use them from then on.

The Lucky Boy contracted a local saw mill to furnish the lumber to build the bunkhouse, mill, cook house, and other miscellaneous buildings needed for their operations. We had a truck on steady hauling lumber and other building materials.

To prepare for the new business, we took delivery of a new Dodge truck to pull the semi, and retired the old 1934 Dodge that had better than 299,000 miles on it. About the same time, the dealer in Blackfoot had a 5-ton 1934 Diamond that they had taken in trade. It needed some engine work and they offered it at such a low price that we decided to try to rebuild its old engine. However, the block was cracked so the only thing we could do was replace the engine. It was a Continental 199 HP with an inline six-cylinder engine and there were not many around. We found a couple, but they were so badly used and priced so high that we knew we would be better off buying a new motor. So we ended up buying a short block, including a new oil pump and water pump. After reconditioning the rest of the parts from the old engine and installing them on the new block, we had practically a new engine. The rest of the truck was in pretty good shape, so after all that we had a heavy-duty truck at a bargain price. And none too soon. We started moving heavy machinery soon after that.

The first job for the new truck was hauling an air compressor for the Forest Service from Challis to the Twin Peaks area where they were building a road, and hauling a disabled Caterpillar tractor from its headquarters in Challis.

Meanwhile Dad, Mr. Dunn, and a crew from the mine were constructing an ore bin down the Lucky Boy Hill where the road from Lucky Boy joins the Yankee Fork road about three miles up the valley from Custer. There would be a road above the bin, so the truck could dump ore into the bin, and another road below so larger trucks could be loaded. Following the same plan, a 2,500-gallon fuel tank would be installed to store oil from a large truck, and below the tank the smaller truck would be able to load. We had a dump bed for the short, 100-inch wheelbase cab-over truck that was being used to pull the van semi-trailer. We used it to haul ore from the mine to the ore bin because it was short enough to negotiate the switchback without backing up. In its place we would use the truck that was pulling the stock trailer to pull the van trailer and use the new Dodge to pull the stock trailer. I made the trip to Boise and brought the big tank to the foot of the hill where it was installed in the place that was prepared for it. The road above the tank was for the big truck with a 2000-gallon tank that could dump its load by gravity. The lower road was for the little truck to fill a 500-gallon tank that fitted in the dump bed to haul up to the mine.

They were getting a space ready to build the mill before the arrival of the machinery. The mill would be built on three levels on the hill. The ore and water were fed in on the top level where the ore was crushed quite fine; then it was fed down into the ball mill along with water, and was further ground by steel balls into a soupy texture. On the lower level, the slurry was fed into the floatation units. They were 4-by-4-by-4 feet with pulleys at the top of a shaft extending down to the bottom of the unit,

Dad, Dutch, and Hilmer

where it was connected to the impellers. The impellers agitated the fluid that contained the powdered ore, water, and chemicals, causing a thick foam that contains the gold and other valuable metals to rise to the top where they are then scraped off into a trough and dried—ready to ship to the smelter.

They needed a lot of cement to make a foundation for all of the heavy machinery, although the floors and building were of wood, as were lots of stairs linking the three levels. We hauled the cement from the cement mill in Inkom to the foot of the Lucky Boy Hill and unloaded it on a dock. Then the small truck would haul as much as it could handle to the mine. The dock was used to transfer all of the freight except the largest and heaviest machinery from the larger trucks to the small one. Even the sand had to be hauled from the riverbed of the Yankee Fork, as there was no sand and gravel on the mountain near the mine. When we had to use bigger trucks, they had to be helped over the steep part of the road by the Cat. Dad ran the small truck and stayed up at the mine. On weekends my brother Dutch would go up and help him, and eventually that became Dutch's job during the summer.

We were given a preview of the machinery that we would be hauling up that hill to the mine. It made one wonder if it could be done. Dad made the remark "don't sit around wondering, figure a way to do it." So, that was the attitude we took.

Meanwhile, a group of buyers were searching the mountains for old ore mills for the scrap iron that was left in them. They contracted with us to haul it out and load it on rail cars in Mackay. The iron that was used in making mining machinery in the 1800s was soft cast iron because welding as we know it today was not yet invented. The only way two pieces of iron could be made into one was for a blacksmith to get them white-hot in a forge and then hammer them together on an anvil until they were one piece. Because welding had become a common practice, soft cast iron hadn't much use any more; so many local folks wondered why these buyers were so eager to buy up these old mills. The old Custer Mill was practically intact when Tuffey McGowan sold it as scrap. He staked out all the old mining properties that appeared to be abandoned, but a lot were private property and absentee owners were paying taxes. If the owners showed up and took possession of their property, Tuffey would try to collect money from them, claiming he was protecting their interest while they were gone. I never heard of him being successful at that. Too many people knew him too well. Mr. Dunn made Tuffey understand that he had no rights in the Lucky Boy whatsoever. They had a real falling out and from then on Tuffey held a grudge against anyone who worked at the Lucky Boy, including the Lindburgs. Dunn even got the post office moved from Tuffey's place in Custer to Sunbeam. That really rubbed salt in the wound.

Some History Destroyed

The biggest loss to the area, I think, was the tearing down of the old Custer Mill. There was pilfering of some small things by visitors who carried them off for souvenirs. Even the big iron cyanide tanks that stood on the flat below the mill were cut up and sold. They were a perfect example of early day construction, showing how they were riveted together before modern day welding. It was said that the iron sheets were brought in small pieces by pack mules and horses and then assembled where they were to be used. Even the timbers and the lumber that housed the mill were hauled off or burned. If that historic old mill were left standing, it would be one of the most interesting historic museums in all of Idaho that was readily accessible to the public.

The Forest Service was just as guilty as anyone for destroying historic buildings and areas. During the 1960s they planned to put everything back to its natural state. The thing I miss the most was the old Yankee Fork Store that was located about 100 yards west of the present store. The Lindburgs have fond memories of that old store, I suppose, because that's where we headquartered in that area. The Forest Service also destroyed other areas, I was told.

There were quite a few people living in Custer in those days and there were a couple of businesses—a beer joint, located in the old Mackenzie Saloon, and a gas station that had a few picnic supplies. A few other buildings that were still standing had people living in them. An old carpenter lived in the old jail and while he was living there, it burned down. In the lower Custer was China Town. It had a few old buildings still standing. Bonanza had a beer joint. The old hotel was occupied and also the Reed residence that is fenced and well maintained. The Reeds still live there in the summer. Some old miners still live in the old mining camp year round, making a living highgrading ore from the old mines. In the summer, the place was swarming with people trying to make money by panning, mining, logging, or finding work in some of the mines that were running.

There were very few tourists in those days, as money was too scarce to spend on travel or vacation. The government had a commodity program and distributed free staples such as sugar, flour, beans, lard, etc. The really destitute might get some relief from the county that issued vouchers for staples and staples only. But most counties were broke, so the merchants had to wait their turn to get paid for the vouchers.

Then there was the county poor farm that some took advantage of, but they were mostly retired folks. Those who were able worked at growing vegetables and some did the canning. The poor farm was located at the Challis Hot Springs, which was like a resort. The hot water was also used to heat the buildings. In those days, people on relief were so ashamed they did everything to keep it a secret. We used to go swimming the in hot water pool at the Challis Hot Springs and I was very impressed with the freshly painted buildings and well-kept grounds of the Custer County poor farm. A lot of people used the hot water pool and the money generated from that helped support the farm. I understood that all medical services at the farm were donated by the local doctors.

Hilmer and Dutch—and Athletics

1937 was going pretty fast. Summer was almost over and we would soon lose Dutch and Hilmer as they were going back to school. Dutch had run the small truck up and down the Lucky Boy Hill hauling what couldn't be hauled with larger trucks. We were going to miss those two reliable kids. I'll take a moment and relate the accomplishments of my two younger brothers.

First, Hilmer took up wrestling and all during his high school career he never lost a bout. Most of his matches were uneventful except the last one of his senior year. A kid from

Challis had a very successful year and word was spread around Challis that Hilmer wouldn't have a chance. The eventful night came and the Challis gym was packed. Hilmer's match was the last on the program as they were heavy weights. Hilmer's opponent was a lot bigger than Hilmer. Hilmer weighed 172 lbs. and his opponent about 227 lbs. The bout lasted less than a minute when Hilmer had him pinned and won the bout. The only ones in the crowd who weren't disappointed were those of us from Mackay.

The high point of Hilmer's athletic career was on the Fourth of July 1938—the summer after he graduated from high school. Mackay was always great for celebrating the Fourth of July. That year a boxing ring was set up in the middle of Main Street. In the evenings several boxing matches were scheduled, but the main attraction and the last event was a wrestling match featuring Hilmer and Bob Hammond. Bob Hammond was the son of John Hammond who I hauled cattle for, although I never knew Bob. I guess he was away attending school at the University of Idaho. He was on the wrestling squad there. I don't know what universities were in that division in those days. When he graduated, he was billed Collegiate Champion of the Northwest and had never lost a match. He later became the athletic coach for Mackay High School. They were a good match up as they were the same size and about the same weight.

The Fourth arrived. A rodeo was held during the day and that night the boxing and wrestling were followed by a big dance. The wrestling was billed as the big event with two undefeated champions. The difference was one was a young high school champ and the other was an older collegiate champ. The rules were two out of three falls. They wrestled, it seemed, for hours. Neither could throw the other and after what seemed like ages, they called the match a draw. So, we still had two completely exhausted champions. Hilmer was so tired he went

Dutch and Edythe

home, took a bath, and went to bed. Bob told Dad that was his toughest match ever. It took him a couple of days to recover.

Leland Duane Lindburg was better known as Dutch. In high school his athletic career was in basketball. He was very good at it due to his 6-foot-3-inch height. He was quite a hustler and an excellent shot and was generally high point man for his team, although they didn't win the division championship. They came very close to winning it in his junior and senior years. I used to go and watch them play whenever possible. It was thrilling to watch them and give him support—as if he needed it. I never knew my dad to attend a game or sport that we played, but I know he was proud of our accomplishments. He often would remark that someone had told him of our excellent play or in the case of Hilmer, how quick and strong he was. Dad always said it was the ten-gallon milk cans he handled all those years.

The Marmon Harrington Truck

We were still preparing to move the heavy machinery up the hill to the Lucky Boy Mine. Someone told Dad of the Marmon Harrington Company that was making four-wheel drives on Ford trucks. Dad contacted them. They were very busy and could not get to us until the spring of 1939, but they had a loaner that we could have until they got one built for us. Well, Dad ordered one and we received the loaner in December of 1938. It was equipped with a four-cylinder Hercules diesel engine. The truck with all wheels driving would go up Lucky Boy Hill without a problem if we didn't load too heavy. So, the short-wheelbase Ford was still the workhorse of running the hill. The diesel engine was sure no asset because it was so hard to start in cold weather. Sometimes, it could take three to four hours to get it running. One time it took all day to start it. Diesel engines hadn't been used much in trucks in those days because they were so heavy. This light one was one of the very first installed in a light truck like this Ford. It was experimental and some changes had to be made. It had its good features. It had a lot of torque and on long steady grades, you didn't have to shift as much, but it was difficult to haul heavy loads on steep grades. In those days, a gas engine was still the best. But, diesels are much improved and are very popular in today's trucks—both light and heavy. I might add that this loaner truck was a cab-over, which made it more difficult to work on and to start. We let it stand and idle quite a bit. It would stand there and shake like it was cold and shivering. The truck that Dad ordered was also a cab-over but it would have a gasoline engine. That Marmon Harrington turned out to be very useful in snow and other places where more traction was needed.

Dad's Chilling Experience

The winter of 1938–1939 was very cold and snowy on the Upper Salmon and the Yankee Fork. A couple nights got down to 50 degrees below zero. When it gets below -35 degrees it is very hard on both man and machinery. When the metal gets that cold, it loses tensile and kind of crystallizes and breaks easily. That's the reason it was wise to warm the transmissions and differentials before you tried to move the truck—which doesn't always solve the problem either. Also, the grease turns to a solid and doesn't lubricate moving parts and that can cause real problems. This is what happened to Dad one cold frosty evening.

The temperature was about 40 below when an axle broke on one of the Ford trucks. He was about a quarter of a mile below the Sunbeam Hot Springs and a mile from the Sunbeam Store. He said his face was nearly frozen when he got to the store. There is a danger that you could frost your lungs. You need to take care and keep your face well covered and don't stay out in the cold for too long a period. When Dad got to the store he called Mackay and asked me to bring him another axle. We happened to have a couple in stock so I left the next morning for Sunbeam in a 1938 Nash that we had traded the Plymouth for. It had a better heater than cars of previous years—although the windshield and windows frosted up. I got to Sunbeam about eight o'clock and the sun was still behind the mountain. In the dead of winter the sun shines in the valley for a short time during the day. It was well below minus 40 degrees. I picked up Dad and we went up to the truck. We had a blowtorch that we were going to use to warm the rear end grease so the axle and stub would come out more easily, but we couldn't keep it running. It was so cold that the generator would cool off and the fire would go out. Then it would squirt raw gasoline. So, we had to resort to the fire pots of sawdust and fuel oil to warm up the transmission and rear differential. Soon we had the axle stub out. We had to install the new axle to start the engine. The hot springs were close by and we had a five-gallon can. The springs put up a cloud of steam you wouldn't believe, but I got my can of water and made it back to the truck. I poured it into the radiator and opened the petcock at the bottom of the radiator so the hot water would run through slowly. Then I went after another can of water. After pouring the second can into the engine, it started right up. It was a good thing as I was nearly frozen. I was wearing a scarf over my face and it was really uncomfortable. We did leave the car engine running so we could climb in and warm up once in a while. It took us most of the morning to get the truck going again. I thought I would never get warm.

Mining in the Winter

The miners who worked the Lucky Boy underground were not affected by the weather because the temperature in the mine was pretty constantly warm in the winter and cool in the summer. They only felt the cold as they were going from the mine to the bunkhouse or the dining hall. So, their production was about the same the year around. When they filled the ore bins, the mine boss would have the road plowed out down the hill so our truck could fill the ore bin at the foot of the hill. They generally did this on a Friday. If the men who worked at the mine got away once in a while, they hardly ever got further than the Sunbeam Store where they stocked up on tobacco. Their families sent them clothes. Anything else that they needed they could get at the Sunbeam Store. Sometimes, if they were from the valley or someplace else that our trucks went, they would ask us to pick up clothes or other things that they needed. We would make the most of the plowed-out roads to move the ore to the rail cars in Mackay, or in the case of high-grade ore, on to the Salt Lake smelters. It was cold every place we went, but the Upper Salmon was the coldest. The Lucky Boy was about the only mine that shipped ore that winter.

During the summer and fall there was a crew getting out mine timbers and firewood for the winter months. They used a lot of firewood for the bunkhouse, the kitchen, and the dining hall. The cook generally stayed in camp all winter. There was always someone to feed. She always had a man, who was known as the bull cook, to do the heavy work—such as splitting the wood and starting the fires in the mornings, so when she got to the kitchen everything was warm and ready for cooking. There was also a second cook to help with things such as waiting tables, doing general housekeeping, and helping with the dishes. The women's quarters was just off of the dining hall. The restroom was a small building about 50 feet from the kitchen and dining hall and was generally referred to as a back house. I never heard of one being heated. There was a water coil in the range so when there was a fire in the range, it heated the water that was then stored in a 50-gallon hot water tank for washing dishes and so forth. Also, a shower was provided in a shower room for the ladies. The bunkhouse also had a boiler fired by wood that furnished hot water for the men to shower and wash up. A washing machine was furnished for washing clothes.

The weather was warming up although there wasn't much thawing as of yet. But the roads stayed open longer than they did a couple of weeks before. I forgot to mention the CCC camp at Bonanza kept the road open to Sunbeam, although very few cars were used up there that winter.

We soon learned that winter wasn't over yet for us. If I remember right, Dad and Dutch took a load of mining supplies into the Yellowjacket Mine. The Yellowjacket is located way back in the wilderness. To get there you went ten miles down Highway 93 below Challis, then over Morgan Creek Summit down to Camas Creek. It is about 50 miles in to the mine from the highway at Morgan Creek, and the mine is located 15 miles up to the head of Camas Creek. The road stays on the south slope of the canyon, which is bare of trees and brush. The entire hillside is composed of very fine shale rock. A wooden flume was used in the summertime to carry water to a small ranch at the mouth of the canyon.

It generally took a long day to make a trip to the mine and back. But Dad and Dutch didn't get back the first day or the second day. Mom became worried and called the O'Conner Ranch (Mrs. O'Conner generally knew everything that went on in that vast area) but she had heard nothing of Dad and Dutch. The O'Conner's phone was the only phone in the area except for the one at the mine. And there was no answer at the mine. Mom was really worried when they didn't show up on the third day. She couldn't get any news on the telephone. The morning of the fourth day she called me to the house and we decided that I should go in and try to find them. I was the only one around that morning, so it was up to me to get everything ready to go. I decided to take the 1937 Dodge—that's the one that pulled the semi-trailer that made the runs to Utah, so it was well equipped for winter driving. Also, it was a good truck on mountain roads. I left Mackay at eleven a.m. and arrived in Challis at noon. I ate a big dinner and headed for the Yellowjacket Mine. I hadn't gotten five miles down the road when I met Dad and Dutch coming out. I turned around and called Mom to let her know they were safe and sound and that they should be home in an hour or so. It wasn't really clear to me why they were delayed so long, but as I remember they said that they were trapped between two snow slides, so they walked back to the mine—even though more slides could have covered the truck. At the mine they were out of danger. The mine had a Caterpillar tractor so it cleared the slides, but it was a slow process. The slides were huge, and because the road was so near the bottom of the canyon, there was no place to push the debris that came down with the slides. The telephone at the mine didn't work because the slides took out the telephone line. After the excitement, everything turned out all right.

The Bingham Canyon Snow Slide

The American Smelting Company obtained an interest in the Yellowjacket Mine. The Yellowjacket used to be a very productive mine and, I guess, there was reason to believe it could still be. The American Smelting and Refining Company had a couple of smelters—one in Washington, one in Utah, and several others I wasn't aware of. The one I hauled to was in the Bingham Canyon south of Salt Lake City.

Bingham Canyon had the world's largest open-pit mine. It was a copper operation. To me it was awesome. It was terraced on the south slope from approximately a quarter from the bottom of the canyon to the top of the mountain. Each terrace was wide enough to accommodate a full-sized railroad that could handle full-sized open-top railcars. They were loaded with big mechanical shovels powered by electricity. Each car held 20 tons of ore. The cars were moved by electric locomotive and assembled into a train at a switchyard near the head of the canyon—then moved to the mill and smelters. Further up the canyon, American Smelting and Refining Company was developing a property called Armstrong Tunnel. I was sent there to get a load of pipe and deliver it to the Yellowjacket. I left Salt Lake City about eleven a.m., hoping to get loaded and back the same day. But, that was not to be. I felt lucky to get out of there alive.

Because of the heavy snow that year, a few warm days made the hillside very unsteady. I had just made it to the Armstrong property when I was informed that a huge snow slide had just come down behind me and that it had covered several occupied houses. In the narrow part of the canyon, most of the dwellings were built back in the hillside with just the front doors and windows exposed out. Where the canyon was wider, full-sized houses were built—a lot of them made of brick. It was reported that about 40 feet of snow had slid into the canyon.

The force of the snow was so great that it brought down full-sized railcars full of ore. It was feared that several people perished and was rated as a major disaster and, as it turned out, their fears were right. Rescue crews were dispatched and they worked all through the night and for the next 48 hours. They used long steel rods that they would push down through the snow. When it struck something soft, they presumed it was a body and most of the time they were right. In the course of three days, it was said they recovered 80 bodies.

Although the upper edge of the slide was well below the Armstrong Tunnel, I was having my problems. The customs and diet there were so different that there was hardly anything I could eat. When I heard about the slide I went to the only little store around to get a loaf of bread and a bottle of milk. No bread—how about crackers. Okay, but no milk. Lots of beer and plenty of water, which was not very satisfying. I passed on the beer, as it would not agree with the stomach trouble I was having. Soon a man came and took me to the boarding house where most of the men ate and some of them slept. I was introduced to the lady who seemed to be the boss—she was big enough to be the boss. She said the evening meal would be in about a half hour and that sounded good to me. I was getting hungry. When the evening meal was served, it was a disappointment. It consisted of boiled potatoes that, with plenty of butter, I could eat. But, the sauerkraut and tripe I had to pass up. After we ate she had a man show me where I would be sleeping. We went up some stairs that were on the outside of the building on the same contour as the hillside, so the upper floor was at ground level. The room had a single light globe, but a very nice warm bed. I slept with my clothes on—what little sleeping I did—and left the light on all night. I made sure that my winter jacket and flashlight were close by. I spent two more nights like that. The next morning I was sure hoping breakfast would be something I could eat. Sure enough, there were corn flakes. I poured a big bowl of them and got some milk when it came around. It was hot, and the corn flakes wilted into a soggy mess. I put sugar on them and ate them anyway.

The next morning, the boss said that we would load the pipe, which was covered with four feet of snow. They took a small Cat tractor and plowed a place for my truck next to the pile of pipe and dug out the pipe by hand. There were five men digging. The first two feet was wet snow, the next foot was the color of water—half snow and half water, and the last foot or less was like solid ice. They used picks to get the pipe out. I had to move the truck to a lean-to and load five tons of mine rail and spikes. After they finished probing for bodies, they started to open the road from the lower end. The boarding house was just about out of food and the little store had closed a couple of days before—ran out of beer, I guess.

The morning of the fourth day the road was open and I started out. There was a lot of traffic bringing the supplies for the upper end of the canyon that was above the slide. As I traveled down the canyon road, especially where the canyon widened out, I saw more destruction than I had ever seen I my life. Entire houses and buildings were completely destroyed with parts of houses scattered in the snow. Only the bottom story remained of one brick building (it could have been two or three stories) and it appeared as if it had been sawed off with a saw, it was sheared so clean.

Down in the mouth of the canyon, where the terrain opens up as the canyon joins the Great Salt Lake Valley several miles below the lake, there is a settlement of very neat houses that were mostly built alike. I suppose the mine company owned them. I never noticed if there were any commercial buildings there or not. But one thing you would notice if you visited there would be that the roofs of every building are of shining copper.

The name of the little town is Copper Town[10]. I say little but I suppose the town had about 1,500 residences. I was held up there by a funeral procession—for victims of the slide, I supposed.

I arrived in Salt Lake City in the late afternoon, parked the truck in the garage we contracted to park our trucks, got a room in the hotel where we generally stayed, and took a bath. The bathroom was down the hall and served several rooms. Sometimes you had to wait your turn. But I was lucky—it was not being used. After cleaning up, I went to a restaurant close by and had a plate of ham and eggs, then went back to the hotel and went to bed. The keys to the rooms were similar and most any key would open the door so I always propped a chair against the door. I really slept that night. I woke up about five the next morning and went for another plate of ham and eggs. As I had no other business in Salt Lake City, I took off for Mackay. I stopped in Pocatello and saw Geryl. He was loaded with general freight and Dewey was loading freight for a CCC camp at Rock Creek. We had lunch at Kelley's on Fifth Street and then Geryl and I traveled together to Mackay. The road across the Arco Desert was in terrible shape. The snow and ice had built up on the pavement and in places it melted down to the pavement and in other places it hadn't, so it was extremely rough—and slow going. It was nearly six p.m. when we arrived in Mackay. The folks were worried about me for the four days I was behind the slide. Communications had broken down and they had no word about me until I called them from Salt Lake City.

The next morning I left for the Yellowjacket Mines to deliver the load I had picked up in Bingham at the Armstrong

---

[10] Copperton, Utah

Tunnel. I had a helper with me that day, a fellow named Doug McIntosh. We made it over the Morgan Summit okay and past O'Conner Ranch, but the road from there to the mine wasn't made for a semi. The only reason we took the semi was because of the long pipe. I was fortunate to have Doug along to throw the rocks that had rolled from the thawing hillside, off of the road. It looked like we would be late getting back so I called Mrs. O'Conner to see if we could have supper there. She said okay and asked what time we would be there—then added "never mind, you'd only be guessing anyway." More rocks had rolled down on the road. Doug estimated he had thrown five tons of rocks that day. We got to O'Conner's about six, had our supper (she sure was a good cook), then left for Mackay. That turned out to be an 18-hour day. We were so late; we went to bed in the truck terminal—Doug in one bed and me in the other.

It was about nine a.m. when the noise out on the loading dock woke me up. I got up, as much as I hated to, got dressed, and went out to see what was going on. A couple of employees were loading my truck with bags of ore. There were four different lots from four different shippers. Because the roads were opening up, these miners' winter work of highgrading allowed small shipments of ore. The sampling mill in Salt Lake City determined the value of each shipper's ore and then bought the ore at that value, less their fee. Then the sampling mill sent the whole lot to the smelters as one shipment. It was cheaper than the smelter trying to deal with each small shipper.

I was at the sampling mill one time when a fellow from the firm that takes care of the sewers for Salt Lake City came in with a load of black sand. He said that sometimes it contains considerable gold and that often they find expensive jewelry, such as gold rings, etc.

The Making of Salt Blocks

The back haul that trip was block salt headed for the Challis Cattlemen Association from the Morton Salt Company. It was fascinating to see how the blocks were made. First, they pump the water from Salt Lake into large ponds and as the water evaporates, the residue is kiln-dried and ground real fine—just like dust. Then it is poured into molds that have one end a little larger than the other. Finally, the molds are placed in a huge press that exerts several tons of pressure. Salt sure makes a lot of noise as it is being squeezed. I didn't think you could squeeze anything dry like that into such a solid form. It would take a solid blow with a hammer to even chip it. Each block weighed 50 pounds. I loaded up the block salt and headed for home. It was a very uneventful trip.

Back to the Mines

I got home in the middle of the afternoon and Dad was waiting for me. The road up the Lucky Boy Hill was drying out and he wanted to send two trucks to Boise. The mine was very eager to get the machinery installed and get the mill running. The salt was unloaded onto the dock. The truck was serviced, getting it ready to go to Boise. The Diamond T was all ready to go and Dad wanted to drive it. Jack Monarch was to drive the Dodge with the semi I had just brought from Salt Lake City. Dewey was delivering freight to the CCC camps in Paul and Rock Creek—then he was to go to Boise for a load of blasting powder.

Jack and I started early the next morning—we were to load at Burroughs place of business. We got to Boise in time to load the ball mill on the Diamond T. It weighed twelve-and-a-half tons with liners. Although they were not installed, they were loose on the truck. Dewey arrived just about time to go eat.

There was a restaurant about a block and a half from where we were loading our trucks. We had never eaten there before and decided to try it. After the states required chauffeur licenses, we were required to wear headgear and display our license on the left side of our headgear. The Lindburg Truck Line chose blue chauffeurs' caps with the name "Lindburg Truck Line" embroidered across the front of the cap and, of course, the license was pinned on the left side. While we were eating, every time I looked up this waitress was looking at me. This was happening often and I began to feel a little uncomfortable. She finally came over to the counter where I was eating and said that she noticed the name on my cap and asked if my name was Roland Lindburg. Then she asked if I went to school in Danbury, Nebraska. I answered yes to both questions. It turned out that she was Floy Fisher, a second grade classmate before we moved back to Idaho. She told me of another second grade classmate who had moved to Boise and who was working for the postal department. His name was Armond Allen. However, I never had a chance to look him up.

We finished loading the next morning. Dewey had to go out of town to the powder house to load the dynamite. We hauled the dynamite from Boise because Mr. Burroughs was the distributor for the Hercules Powder Company in the state of Idaho and he sure wasn't going to buy powder for a mine that he had a financial interest in from someone else. The closest route from Boise to the Lucky Boy Mine is through the Wood River, Ketchum, over Galena Summit, down the Salmon River to the Yankee Fork, then up to the mine. However, Galena Summit was unimproved with such a long pull and so many switchbacks; it was more feasible to go through Lost River, over Willow Creek Summit, then over Spar Canyon, down the East Fork of the Salmon to the main Salmon to the Yankee Fork, then to the mine.

When we reached the foot of the road to the Lucky Boy Mine at the Fourth of July Creek, the dynamite was unloaded on the dock and was hauled up to the mine in the small dump truck. The floatation units were taken up the hill on the new Marmon Harrington truck. It took two loads but it worked real well. Now, the Diamond T had to take its own load up. I had to back a little to get around from the Fourth of July Creek to the Custer side of the ridge—then straight to the 32 percent grade. Dad wanted to see if the Marmon Harrington would have enough power and traction to help the Diamond T up the grade. The Diamond T had a 15-ton load and several men with blocks to block the wheels if we couldn't make it. But, we made it just fine. Was Dad ever delighted.

The year of 1939 was one of steady growth for the truck line. Geryl was staying in Pocatello most of the time picking up shipments to be loaded on trucks going through at night or evenings after the warehouses and wholesale houses closed. He stayed with a family that took in roomers and boarders. Their last name was Sherman. We had a deal with them for our employees to stay there when they had to lay over in Pocatello.

My Brother, Geryl

It's time to describe the life of my brother Geryl. Geryl was my full brother. He was born in Darlington, Idaho on February 2, 1916. Our mother passed away when he was only six months old. For the next three years he, with me, was cared for by our grandmother and aunts in Polk, Nebraska. He was quite different in several ways than the rest of us boys. He always kept himself well dressed. He was always neat and clean although he did most of the same work the rest of us did. He also helped Mom do some housework. He didn't care much for machinery, although he knew how to operate most of it. I can't remember ever seeing him on the tractor. He would play with girls as well as boys and had lots of friends. Even after our house burned and we were wearing donated clothing, he always wore his clothes well.

Geryl was a very good manager and organizer in his end of the business. He grouped the shipments according to their destination so the nearest customer's order would be to the back of the truck and easy to get off. Geryl was a very good dancer and attended many dances. All of the girls liked to dance with him. He had many girlfriends, but to our surprise, on June 11th he married Ruth Olson, a girl he had known since they were little kids and went to school with. They only lived about a half mile from us when we lived at Darlington. After they were married, they rented a place in Mackay that had extra rooms—one with two beds. I stayed there once in a while, and so did Dutch.

The Shell Oil Company had several contracts to furnish oil and gas to the contractors building the road down the Salmon River. All the gas was shipped in barrels that we would pick up in Arco on our way through from Pocatello or beyond—usually late at night. Ira Boyer, the dealer for Shell Oil, was very good at getting up anytime of the night to load us. But he was always complaining about not getting any of the empty barrels back. We tried to bring the empties back, but were not very successful because the contractors left them wherever they emptied them. Ira had to account for every barrel or be charged for them. So one day he decided to go along with me on a trip up the Salmon River to gather his barrels. That day I had a load going up but would be empty coming back. I didn't get to Arco until late at night on the day he was scheduled to go, but he was there and ready to go anyhow. We decided to spend the rest of the night in Mackay. We planned to use the spare bedroom at Geryl's house but when we got there Dutch was sound asleep in one of the beds. There were only two pillows for the three of us, so we decided to jerk the pillow from under Dutch's head—he was sleeping so hard that he probably would never miss it. When I jerked the pillow, he sat straight up with both arms outstretched and hollered "whoa babe," then laid back down and slept the rest of the night without the pillow.

The next day we found most of Ira's barrels. About five miles out of Mackay, coming down Mackay Dam Hill, we ran into a swarm of bees and, because the day was very warm, we had the windshield tilted out to get more air. As we were traveling at 50 miles per hour, the bees hit us right in the face. I ducked my head down and got a collar full of dead and stunned honeybees. In fact, the whole inside of the cab was a sticky mess—stunned bees crawling all over. We stopped and cleaned them out of the cab. Luckily, we never got a sting.

It wasn't long until Geryl and Ruth moved to Pocatello. He continued gathering freight for us. We had changed to a bigger warehouse for more space. It was owned by Ollie Roach. He also was in the business of storing and moving household goods. He was the agent for Allied Vans that moved household goods. If I remember right, Geryl did some work for Roach in his warehouse in addition to his work with us. He rented a couple of houses in Pocatello. The house in the north part of town was big enough to board a couple of college kids. One was Bob Deires, who was attending Idaho State and gave flying lessons from the Idaho State airfield that was just north of the college. After the war, the college built the large athletic complex that contains the large dome building that houses their football field, track, etc. I think Geryl and Ruth lived there until after the war.

Geryl was a hard worker who was well liked by everyone he worked with or came in contact with. He was also a Mason. People who rode with him or observed his driving declared that he was the best truck driver they had ever seen. He shifted gears so smoothly that it was easy on the engines. During the war he drove an Allied Moving Van nationwide. He always stopped to see us when he was close to where we lived—he even visited Helene and me when we lived in the trailer at Hanford, Washington. He parked his van in front of our trailer and stayed the night. He and Ruth had bought a nice house on West Cedar in Pocatello that he enjoyed for several years. Ruth still lives there.[11]

Geryl accomplished a lot in his short life. He was 47 years old when he passed away. Geryl was sick a lot and was examined by many doctors. They took his appendix out, but he got no relief. After several years of suffering, they found cancer in his colon, removed it, and thought they got it all. Geryl and Ruth had two children: Gary born in 1940 and Sandra in July of 1941. At Dad's funeral in 1963, the five of us siblings had our picture taken. Geryl was feeling all right then, but in the summer he got very sick so we went to see him at their home on West Cedar in Pocatello. He was hurting so bad that after of couple of days we took him to the hospital. After a lot of suffering he passed away in October of 1963. He is buried in the Masons Cemetery in Pocatello.

The Olsons

Ruth's dad, Charley Olson, came to Idaho about the time that Dad and the Carlsons did. He had bought the Darlington place, a well-developed 80 acres with several buildings with domestic water under pressure from a water tower. There were several children in that family, including three who were born

---

[11] 1999.

deaf. Harry was the oldest; then, I'm not sure, but I think there was an older sister, Helen, I never knew. After Harry came Gordon—then Ruby, Calmer, Evelyn (my age), Raymond, Ruth and Josephine. Harry, Ruby, and Evelyn were deaf. They were deaf but very smart. Harry worked in a sawmill near Spokane. Ruby was very pretty and a very good dancer. Evelyn married a barber and lived in Roseburg, Oregon. Charley, their father, died in 1929. He must have been a very good manager to raise a family of that size on 80 acres, although it was one of the best pieces of ground in the valley.

The Summer of 1939

The Depression wasn't getting better and I never saw so many men, some with families, all looking for work, checking every morning at the mines that were operating such as the Lucky Boy, Clayton Silver, and some smaller operations. After checking for work, some would pan for gold in the nearby creeks or highgrade old mines.

The Challis Cattlemen Association would bring thousands of cattle to graze in the Stanley Basin. The cattle grazed in belly-deep grass. There were several cow camps in the basin in the summertime so that meant there were many cowboys around. There were a few bands of sheep in the valley, but I seldom saw a sheepherder, as they generally stayed out with their sheep. With all of the grazing going on, the underbrush was pretty well consumed so we seldom had wildfires in those days. With so many men whose livelihoods depended on a fire-free forest and meadow, everyone was on the lookout for lightning fires and often had a fire out before it could get a good start.

Silas Mason Company

Meanwhile, there was a lot of activity on the Yankee Fork where the valley widens out above Pole Creek. Crews of men were digging holes down to bedrock to determine how much gold was there, just as if someone was going to dredge. It reminded people of the dredge that was moved there in 1934 but never set up. It had people wondering if the owner was coming back. It was quite a mystery. People out there digging holes and then filling them up. By the end of the year, it wasn't a mystery. A new outfit was prospecting. They were people from Silas Mason Company, one of the big six that was constructing the Grand Coulee Dam. The government was offering them a good tax break if they could make jobs as the Depression was not improving.

The superintendent for Silas Mason Company of New York, Mr. Murphy, traveled the northwest quite a bit. In his travels he visited dredges in Montana that were working in very rich ground and were producing lots of gold. He became so interested in the dredge operations that he persuaded the company to do some looking around to find some available ground for prospecting. They looked at and tested several places in Idaho and Nevada. Then they heard about a big piece of land under a single ownership on the Yankee Fork. I guess they determined there was enough gold.

They asked several dredge manufacturers to come look at the ground and give them a price of a dredge that could handle the big boulders that lay under the surface. After looking, only one company decided to build a dredge that could handle the large rocks they would encounter and that would dig 35 feet deep to easily reach bedrock where most of the gold laid. Years before, the Yuba Company had sent a representative to the valley for the dredge company that failed, so they did not send anyone. The Bucyrus-Erie Company sent a representative who, because of the nature of the ground, advised smaller and heavier buckets than usual and a heavier super structure. All together it would have to be heavier than normal for a dredge that size. That seemed to satisfy the company, so in February of 1940 they ordered the dredge.

Silas Mason Company named the operation the Snake River Mining Company and then obtained the ground and all the buildings that the former mining company had put together. They had even dug a pond to assemble the dredge in. Howard Davis got his ice there for the Sunbeam Store. It was just a three-mile haul instead of an eighteen-mile haul from Little Redfish Lake. As soon as they had ordered the dredge they asked Dad if he could haul it from the end of the railroad to the dredge site—which was the same route we used to haul the 1934 dredge. He was advised that some parts would weigh up to 30 tons. We had no truck that could haul that heavy a load, but we supposed we could build up the six-year-old Diamond T so it could handle that kind of load. So, the next time I had it in Boise, I took it to a place that did that kind of work. They said it could be done so I asked them to do it. I rode back to Mackay with Hilmer, who had a load of supplies for the Lucky Boy Mine. When they called and said that they had it done, we went down to get it. It didn't look like the same truck. They had fished-plated the frame so it was about twice as heavy. They extended the frame, put another set of dual wheels behind the drivers, and made a ten-wheeler out of it. What they couldn't fix was the road we had to travel. Although the new road was finished down to the mouth of the East Fork, there was no road from East Fork to Challis that we could use because the bridge couldn't handle the heavy loads. It still was a one-lane road with turnouts so we had to use the Spar Canyon road, which had no bridges but had some sharp turns. Going up the canyon was quite a steep pull. Then there was a narrow mountain road for about ten miles to the new road, and then new bridges the rest of the way to the dredge site.

We thought we were ready as Dad had bought a new 1939 long-wheelbase ten-wheeler. He thought he had a bargain as the dealer had it on the lot for over a year and it didn't sell. It turned out to be a very good truck.

Helene

Once in a while someone would ask me how I met my wife. All I could say was I never met her—I always knew her. I had known the Tschanzes for a long time. She was just a little kid down in grade school; just one of the Tschanz kids. I knew she was going to college in Pocatello, but never gave it another thought. Then one Friday, I stopped at the garage where we always fueled and parked our trucks. I was coming through from Salt Lake City and, as I was gassing my truck, the station attendant said a young lady from the college called and said she would like a ride to Mackay. The young lady was Helene. She had changed so much that I hardly recognized her. I couldn't believe it. We then dated a couple of times while she was in college. The lady who was in charge of the dormitory made me understand that Helene was to be in by midnight. We began to see each other quite often.

The San Francisco World's Fair

Things slacked up a little so Dutch, Jim and Earl McAffee, and I decided to go to the World's Fair in San Francisco. McAffee's sheepherder wanted to go too, so there were five of us. Dutch and I started with $400 each. We shared gas expenses. The sheepherder was drunk at every stop we made. We stopped for the night in Las Vegas, Nevada, which was a very small town at that time. It had only a small cabin court with shelter between cabins for cars, only one gambling joint with mostly horse betting, a few card tables, and a couple of crap tables. I cashed my first traveler's check there. They didn't believe in paper money, as they were known as the Silver State. They gave me 20 silver dollars. I put 10 in each front pocket. Boy, was I loaded down. The next day we went to Boulder where the Hoover Dam was being built. That was where the action was. They had cables stretched clear across the canyon that were strong enough to lower a loaded railroad car from the top of the canyon to the bottom where the material was needed. The dam was about half built when we were there. Then we went on to the fair. After that we went down to Los Angeles sightseeing and out to Catalina Island to look around. We arrived at Catalina about ten a.m. when the ships docked. The water was very clear and kids would dive to the bottom for pennies thrown by the tourists. We took a ride in a glass-bottom boat to view the different colored fish. We went to the famous ballroom. It was a sight to watch the dancers and see their images on the black marble floor—just like a mirror, only black.

At nine p.m. we boarded a ship back to Los Angeles. A heavy wind came up and the sea got very choppy, then big waves followed. A ship north of us would sometimes appear to be way above us and then would appear to dip way below us. As the ship would go down between the waves you got the feeling you were weightless. The ship was going down faster than my stomach. That was the closest I ever got to being seasick. A guy next to me handed me a lemon drop and said to suck on this and go to the middle of the ship. It calmed my stomach right down. Not so with Dutch and Jim. I don't believe I ever saw two guys as sick as they were the next day. As we traveled on the road along the ocean, we were headed for home. We got to Reno the second night and did a little gambling. I didn't win anything and still had $30 when I got home.

Business as Usual

The rest of the year went as usual—hauling cattle, ore, cattle feed and mine supplies, and trips to the CCC camps. One of the camps was located on the West Fork of the Yankee Fork (where we parked our trailer while we were restoring the dredge in the 1980s). The camp had a very good doctor who treated not only the CCC boys but also anyone else who needed treatment for illness or accident. Several people who couldn't find work left the camp, and the families who were panning for gold also left so their kids could go to school.

Marj, the wife of Otto Jr., said in 1999 that she met him in 1939. I thought Otto Jr. was still working for us when we hauled the dredge in 1940, because he drove into the ditch just below Mackay and tipped over the new Ford ten-wheeler with a load of general freight. I thought he left us later that year. Anyway, I remember he told us that he had an offer from the Garrett Freight Line but really didn't want to leave us. Dad told him he had better take it, so he did. What none of us knew at the time was that Clarence Garrett had talked to Dad about Otto's ability to create tariffs and his proficiency at other duties that are essential to a good transportation system.

That winter, there was a heavy snow in the Yankee Fork. All operations were shut down except the Lucky Boy Mine and Mill and the CCC camp that kept the road passable. Some of the trucks were idle most of the time so we did a lot of repair work on them. The Snake River Mining Company had one man hired and he was the watchman. The Galena Summit was closed. Everything had to come up the river. I think the road was open as far as Nerridean, but I'm not sure about that.

I remember that Hilmer was married the last of January. He married Zelma Bitton. I don't think she went to school in

Mackay.[12] The family moved to a ranch below town from Moreland, Idaho. She and Hilmer were the same age. Her dad was known as Billy Bitton. They were a large family. Mr. Bitton started an implement business in town just across the street from our truck headquarters.

The Big Haul

In February we learned that the Snake River Mining Company had ordered a dredge from the Bucyrus-Erie Company. The Olson Company from Boise was to build the pontoons and the frame. Ingersoll-Rand built two 450-horsepower engines that furnished the power to run the dredge. General Electric furnished the two 450-horsepower alternators that were attached to the engines. They also furnished the various electric motors that ran the machinery that made the dredge run. The dredge had very heavy framework and pontoons and relatively small buckets for the size and weight of the framework.

Roland with load from Bucyrus Erie

---

[12] Zelma Bitton graduated from Mackay High School in 1938.

The dredge began to arrive in Mackay the first part of May 1940 in a gondola railcar. When Dad saw that, he went directly to the depot and sent a wire to the Bucyrus-Erie Company to inform them not to send anything else in gondolas—to use flat cars because we had no way to unload gondolas. But as luck would have it, the end of that first gondola would open so we were able to unload the miscellaneous parts, though it was not easy. It took two trucks to haul the first carload. The rest of the parts came on flat cars.

I made a piece of equipment to haul the longer loads. I used the rear assembly of an old truck and heated the right and left frame so they could be formed into a tongue. Then I welded a heavy ring onto the end that fit into a hitch that I bought and mounted on the back of the Diamond T. Then I mounted a fifth wheel on the semi-trailer so it would become a four-wheel trailer and, as it turned out, we needed it with its four extra tires. It was a little crude when compared to the factory-made dollies. We took pictures of the rig when we hauled the spud and swing winches. It took 60 loads to move that dredge into the Yankee Fork from Mackay and it was being assembled as fast as we hauled in the parts.

Probably the most spectacular load we hauled was the spud. The spud was mounted on the back of the dredge in a

Home-made dolly behind the Diamond T

The spud, pulled by the Diamond T

vertical position. It had pulleys that accommodated a series of cables at the top, so it could be raised up in a frame made for that purpose. It was so heavy that when it was released, it would penetrate the ground clear to bedrock. And must have been more than 35 feet long. It had a very heavy solid iron point on it that must have weighed more than three tons. It was so long that it arrived in Mackay on three flat railcars. We moved it from the railcars onto the Diamond T and the four-wheel trailer with pry bars, planks and rollers.

We placed a 12-by-12 eight-foot timber crosswise on the flat bed of the Diamond T and another timber the same size on the trailer. The spud was 3-by-3-by-35 feet long, and we loaded it right in the center of the truck and trailer. We put a chain around it to tie it to the truck—just for looks, I guess. Because it was big and heavy, it couldn't move unless the truck tipped over. We had plenty of spectators watching us load it; especially when the truck started to move. We had right-angle turns to make and there was no traffic, so I swung real wide on both turns and was on the highway. It pivoted on the timbers as we thought it would. I pulled over to the side of the road and waited until evening when it cooled to start the trip. At seven that evening, I started (with a helper) for the dredge that was

85 miles away. Spectators were betting I wouldn't make it. We had no trouble but it was about midnight when we got to the top of Spar Canyon—not yet halfway. At the lower end of the canyon we encountered some very sharp turns. But by staying as wide as possible to keep the trailer from hitting the rock wall and by keeping the truck as close as possible to the rock wall on the inside turns to keep the trailer from running off of the road into the creek bed, we inched along. The last challenge was a very short steep climb just before we got out of the canyon. I used the lowest gear I had and we made it just fine. Going down the East Fork was no problem although the going was very slow because it was the old stage road. After five miles of that we were on the new highway. It didn't take long and we were in Clayton where we stopped for breakfast a little after sunup. We had no trouble until we got to Yankee Fork. As soon as we crossed the Yankee Fork Bridge I needed to swing real wide and line up the truck and trailer for the steep climb up to the Yankee Fork Store. We got about half way up the hill and lost traction. We were stuck. It was after nine o'clock. I kept from rolling back by running the engine and standing on the brakes as hard as I

The completed Yankee Fork Dredge

could while my helper found big rocks to block all of the wheels. It seemed forever before he had them blocked. Meanwhile Dad had just caught up with us. He left Mackay early that morning in the car. As luck would have it, our four-wheel drive truck was parked at the Sunbeam Store. Dad parked the car and walked up to get the truck. With a chain fastened to the front of the Diamond T and with both of the trucks pulling, we finally made it up the grade to the flat road in front of the store.

Word spread that the spud was in and we attracted a crowd. But, we still had five miles of single-track road left with one sharp turn and a small bridge. It was slow, but we had no problems. At last, we were at the dredge site. We made it.

Epilogue

The delivery of the dredge to the Yankee Fork was an important story in Roland's life. Helene's arrival was more so. The two were married in October 1940.

They eventually left Mackay, living first in Cascade, Idaho. Roland found work as a "cat skinner," operating a Caterpillar tractor for Idaho Power during the construction of the power transmission line from Black Canyon Dam in Emmett to the Stibnite Mine complex outside Yellow Pine.

World War II brought changes for Roland and his family, much as it did for the rest of the nation. Mining priorities in Idaho changed overnight, with some mines expanded to supply the war effort, while others were shuttered by lack of fuel and manpower. In early 1944, Roland and Helene moved with their two young children to Hanford, Washington. Tens of thousands of workers were drawn to eastern Washington to work on the Hanford Atomic Project, a secret mission to produce weapons plutonium, ending with an explosion above Japan in 1945. Roland worked as a mechanic, and they all lived in a 20-foot camping trailer.

After a few months, the family settled in nearby Prosser, Washington. In 1949, Roland and Helene started the Lindburg Insurance Agency. Roland found a niche serving the farms created by new, large-scale irrigation projects. Over time, the business grew and provided the means to settle and raise a boy and three girls: Rick, Karen, Joanie, and Bethene.

During the next 30 years, Roland became a community leader, driving the creation of the Benton County Port District, and serving as its first chairman. This government agency attracted the fruit processing industry to Prosser and incubated pillars of the Washington wine industry. He also chaired the annual Prosser States' Day parade for several years.

Roland was a proud barbershop singer; his quartet was the Prosser Pops. He and Helene often traveled to conventions and entertained thousands. He also cut wood, fixed cars, gardened, and leaned to fly airplanes. Most importantly, he made sure his children had the opportunity of a college education.

Roland and Helene were surrounded by family. Their four children and five grandchildren stayed in the Northwest. Helene's parents, Otto and Myra Tschanz, retired to Prosser.

In 1980, Roland attended a reunion of workers of the Yankee Fork dredge, a group that became the Yankee Fork Gold Dredge Association. They worked to restore and protect the abandoned dredge, and invited the public to tour and learn. Through the 1980s Helene and Roland would spend each summer at the "dredge camp," often with a grandchild in tow.

Roland lost Helene to Alzheimer's disease in 1993. With grandchildren grown and with limited mobility, Roland began recording some of the entertaining stories he had so often shared with others throughout his life. He typed them slowly, hunting and pecking, into a word processor.

Roland died in 2000 at age 86. His children and other family members collaborated to publish the first edition of this book in 2005.

Index

McDermott, Pete, 66
McGowan, Tuffey, 133
McIntosh, Doug, 147
Midway, 84, 107, 122
Monarch, Jack, 127, 148
Moore, 27, 43, 70, 83, 107
Moreland, 29, 92, 160
Morgan Creek, 94, 141
Morrison Knudson, 71
Morton Salt Company, 148
Murray, Ilene, 60
Neal, Eva, 26, 40
Neal, Roy, 26
North Fork, Salmon River, 91
O'Conner Ranch, 142, 147
Obsidian, 105
Ogden (Utah), 42, 53, 61, 63, 67, 73, 89, 93, 98, 99, 101, 105, 109
Olson, Charley, 1, 153
Olson, Gordon, 15
Olson, Ruth (Mrs. Geryl Lindburg), 151, 153
Pahsimeroi River, 44, 86, 107, 127
Pahsimeroi Valley, 86, 87, 100
Park City (Utah), 119
Pass Creek CCC Camp, 62, 91, 126, 128
Patterson, 86, 87, 104, 105, 127
Paul CCC Camp, 91, 104, 128, 148
Peach Creek, 98
Pence, Charley, 40
Pence, Glen, 40
Pence, Jim, 35, 40
Pence, Tom, 40
Peterson, Elmer, 124, 127
Phelps, Dr., 63, 64, 93

Made in the USA
Monee, IL
24 December 2024

72132759R00105